Raising Cain

Caring for Troubled Youngsters
Repairing Our Troubled System

written by
Richard J. Delaney, Ph.D.

illustrated by
Terry McNerney

Published by:

Wood & Barnes Publishing
2717 NW 50th
Oklahoma City, OK 73112
(405) 946-0621

Printed in the United States of America
Oklahoma City, Oklahoma
ISBN # 1-885473-17-6

To order copies of this book, please call:
Jean Barnes Books
800-678-0621

To all helping professionals
whose labor of love includes troubled
foster and adopted children.

Acknowledgments

I want to thank the many foster and adoptive parents who
have allowed me into their homes, their lives and their struggles.
Specifically, to Norm and Bonnie, Chris and Glenn, Denice and Paul,
I want to express my gratitude for your insights into your children and
yourselves as foster and adoptive parents. Additionally, I wish to express
admiration for the many creative and candid foster and adoptive parents
I have met in support groups. Your creativity and tenacity in assisting
each other in your loving task is inspirational. Lastly, thanks to the
editorial assistance, proofreading, and general support of the
publishers of this book, and specifically to David Wood.

Richard Delaney
Dillon, MT
January, 1998

Foreward

Even in the midst of the unbearable agonies...,there are those who choose to help - to give to others: bread, shoes, comfort, whatever. These acts of compassion are the shining, diamond-tough confirmations of human dignity. This is keeping our affairs in order at the highest level. This is communion in it's highest form. The ritual of the keeping of the living flame. Held daily in the unfinished cathedral of the human spirit.
Excerpt, From Beginning to End, by Robert Fulghum

I was a little surprised when Rick asked me to write the forward to Raising Cain. I'm a book seller, a publisher, not a peer in the treatment field nor a parent that has waged many years on the uneven terrain of foster and adoptive care. I'm supposed to be writing acknowledgments, not forewards. Why Me? The answer to that may be as simple as the ease with which I referred to Dr. Delaney as Rick in the first sentence. Many of us know "Dr. Delaney", the learned, methodical, workhorse that seems to never tire from his mission to help today's foster and adoptive families discover their own healing power. Even more of us know him as "Rick" the thoughtful, caring and humorous man who has become a virtual clearinghouse for the education of professionals, parents and society in the important issue of foster and adoptive care.

This book by Rick, our friend and peer, contains what we at Wood 'N' Barnes see as some of his best work to date. Not only does Dr. Delaney share his "take" on the current status of children and families in foster and adoptive care but does so in terms that we can grasp, learn from and be motivated by. His suggestions for review and repair often confront and challenge systemic problems that are taken for granted as unchangeable. Rick tackles these issues head on and then illustrates in his usual humorous and insightful way the tragedy and the triumph of the problems and their potential resolution.

The problem of children in limbo....

....One dilemma of today's society, often neglected and misunderstood, certainly has many faces. The face that Dr. Delaney defines for us, and many of you live with, isn't often pretty. However, in Raising Cain, Rick offers us not only a new foundation for the issues of foster and adoptive care, but innovative treatment strategies that are far from cosmetic.

He reminds us that the faults inherent to "the system" are reparable, and that those of us entrusted with the multifaceted process of care-giving for our troubled foster and adopted children CAN alter the system. We CAN expedite court decisions, we CAN develop innovative programs, create support groups as well as initiate and emphasize the importance of respite care.

Join Rick in this amazing, timely and challenging presentation!

David Wood
Publisher

Preface

As we know from the Bible, Cain was the first emotionally disturbed child. Insanely competitive with his brother Abel, Cain committed the first homicide. For his crime, an indelible mark was placed upon Cain setting him apart from all others. And, as the story goes, he was banished to wander, to drift, alone and marked for life. Wherever Cain went, he was *persona non grata*.

Cain is a metaphor for today's troubled foster and adopted children. These unfortunate youngsters, in a sense, are our modern "Cains" - not in the specifics of his crime, but in their disturbance, wandering, drifting and inability to be part of the family.

Few troubled foster or adoptive children were raised in Paradise. In fact many were brought up in a godless terrain, lacking compassion, direction and love. Their early years were spoiled by premature loss of innocence, by abuse, neglect and sexual exploitation. In some instances, like Cain, these children are marked forever by crimes (e.g. other's crimes) in their past.

Today's foster and adopted children are an imperiled group. Most have endured upheaval, dislocation, and maltreatment which has assailed their sense of security, worth and identity. The size of this group is reaching biblical proportions. Despite efforts to avert out-of-home placement, the number of foster children continues to swell in the United States and Canada. Naturally, this is also true for those special needs children waiting for adoptive homes.

By report of foster and adoptive parents, the children placed in their care arrive with problems so severe, many become unmanageable within the family setting and in the community. These unmanageably disturbed foster and adoptive children frequently wander via "foster care drift" because no one can contain them, reach them, or successfully make them part of a family.

In years past, this troubled group of youngsters would have found itself in psychiatric hospitals, state facilities, or residential treatment centers for a stay of several months up to several years. However, today's troubled youth are more frequently

Children receiving care in residential or institutional settings are removed after a nominal stay.

frequently found in foster or adoptive families. While some family placements survive, many falter or fail, once again sending the child to wander.

The massive welfare system overhaul, combined with the quest to manage health care costs, threatens an already jeopardized group - troubled foster and adopted children. In crises, children are hospitalized in psychiatric units, but are quickly medicated and returned to the community without adequate observation and evaluation. Children receiving care in residential or institutional settings are removed after a nominal stay and quickly placed within foster homes without supports in place to ensure successful outcomes. In the interests of cost-cutting, children who would have remained in therapeutic foster home placement are allowed increasingly shorter periods of time to stabilize. If they have not been "cured" in twelve months, for example, they are merely demoted to regular foster care, or, in some instances, sent back to the family of origin.

The supports for troubled foster children have been sharply cut and the intensive care furnished by psychiatric inpatient and residential treatment centers has been all but eliminated. We have erected, in effect, a "psychiatric children's hospital without walls" on the backs of foster and adoptive parents, agency workers, traditional school systems, and outpatient mental health professionals. Are these individuals ready for the task ahead of them? Can foster and adoptive families handle the level of disturbance found in the youngsters placed in their care? Can communities sustain children with very significant emotional and behavioral problems? Can we reach these children and end their wandering and drifting? Returning to our biblical metaphor - can we offer Cain a family once again?

Overview of the Book

Raising Cain consists of six chapters. **Chapter One** focuses upon the characteristics of troubled foster and adopted children and upon fourteen hallmark behavioral problems which they often display.

Chapter Two discusses the impact of raising a troubled child in the foster and adoptive family. Special emphasis is placed on an explanation of why foster and adoptive mothers are so predictably victimized by disturbed children in their care.

In **Chapter Three** we introduce a new model for the delivery of mental health services to troubled foster and adopted children and their families. Additionally, we underscore the importance of interpreting the underlying meaning of behavioral problems. Further, we provide a comprehensive collection of questions which guide the process of building healing strategies.

Chapter Four describes sixteen sample family-based strategies which address behavioral problems and related underlying issues.

In **Chapter Five** we critique and confront five national trends in programs and practice which threaten the interests of foster and adopted children and their families.

Lastly, ending on a positive note, **Chapter Six** highlights five crucial ways by which we can better protect the interests of troubled foster and adopted children and their families.

TABLE OF CONTENTS

There's an old maxim, "The same fire that melts the butter, tempers the steel."
Too many of our young, troubled Cains are melted butter.

ONE

The Children: Troubled Like Cain, Marked by Their Past

A decade ago foster and adopted children were a mix of functional and dysfunctional, disturbed and undisturbed youngsters. For every troubled Cain, there was an untroubled Abel. In those days some, but not all, of those placed in foster or adoptive homes were special needs children with serious emotional and behavioral problems. In those times, many of them had been spared extreme trauma, chronic maltreatment, fetal alcohol and drug effects and/or sexual abuse. However, the placement into foster homes of essentially healthy children, from families with mild, temporary troubles, is a thing of the past, seemingly as ancient as the Old Testament, as lost as the Garden of Eden. In the past there were some foster children who were tempered by the adversity they had come from. However, many of today's foster children experience a psychological meltdown from the grave maltreatment they have endured.

There's an old maxim, "The same fire that melts the butter, tempers the steel." Too many of our young, troubled Cains are melted butter. Others are hardened, but not tempered, not truly strengthened by adversity, trauma and abuse. We can tell these melted or hardened youngsters by common signs and symptoms, fourteen of which we enumerate next:*

1. Eating Disorders
2. Vengeful Expression of Anger
3. Feeling of Being a Victim
4. Inability to Profit from Experience
5. Stealing
6. Chaotic Behavior
7. Revolving Scapegoat Behavior
8. Non-communicativeness
9. Emotional Immaturity
10. Sense of Entitlement

11. Family Phobia
12. Lying
13. Self-parenting
14. Loss sensitivity

In this chapter we will illustrate each of the fourteen markers which typify children who have come to foster care or adoption with unfortunate histories. Many disturbed youngsters will show only a few or several of the symptoms, while occasionally some children will manifest all fourteen signs, particularly if they have been maltreated chronically and have suffered multiple separations and losses in their earliest months and years of life.

*Other problem behaviors include: fire-setting, enuresis/encopresis, cruelty to animals, assaultive behavior, truancy, runaway behavior, etc. (Please see Fostering Changes, Appendices.)

For many kids, food has become a fetish, a fixation, a quick fix.

1. Eating Disorders in Foster/Adopted Children

Eating disorders, especially stealing, hoarding and gorging food, run rampant in troubled foster and adopted children. Many foster and adopted children have experienced early neglect, malnourishment, and physical impoverishment - a fundamental let-down from parents who truly could not supply adequate care. Examples of this are glaringly obvious for many children. In one case, an infant was fed bean juice instead of formula or mother's milk. In yet another situation, a foster child stole from the garbage and the dog dish. In still other cases, children adopted from third world orphanages are so sorely under-stimulated and neglected that they experienced failure to thrive, psychological dwarfism, and related developmental delays. These children are often prone to eating disorders.

Lack of nurturing, stimulation, and basic caring - along with the potential for the withdrawal of food for body and soul - results in a sense of emptiness and inner aching. The expectation which develops is that the world does not provide. Faith, the basic trust that care-givers sense the child needs and responds to, accordingly fails to develop.

Without the fullness and sense of true satisfaction which stems from having been loved, many children search for a palpable substitute satisfaction. Food is clearly one avenue. Youngsters may steal and hoard food, they may eat from the dog's dish or out of the garbage can, or they might gorge food until they become physically ill. For many kids, food has become a fetish, a fixation, a quick fix.

The child who harbors secret anger which he refuses to verbalize directly, often acts in angry ways calculated to get back at the family...

2. Vengefulness

Many troubled foster and adoptive children have problems with anger. Some have explosive, violent tempers and "hair-trigger" eruptions, while others dig a hole and bury their anger, withholding it secretly, and then act it out vengefully, later.

Some parents find that it is easier to deal with the child who has a ballistic temper, for at least it is out in the open. The child who harbors secret anger which he refuses to verbalize directly, often acts in angry ways calculated to get back at the family, as in the following case:

The Koblert's were a good foster family with years of experience. They had a very demanding child who needed inordinate amounts of attention, which the family attempted to give in a variety of ways. One way in which all the foster children received individualized attention was through acting as sous-Chef to the foster mother, who gave each child one night a week to assist in the preparation of dinner. On a certain Tuesday, Johnny had his turn to assist and looked forward to it all day (actually he was rubbing the other kids' noses in it). When late afternoon came, he was working side by side with the foster mother in the kitchen. Unfortunately, a call came in from the school - an emergency with one of the other foster children. With apologies to Johnny, Mrs. Koblert drove to school, leaving Johnny to complete the supper under supervision of an older sister...who had attention problems and wandered away from the cooking.

Later, with mother back from school, the family gathered around the dinner table and ate the stew which Johnny had prepared, almost single-handedly. He wore a Cheshire grin as the family ate bowl after bowl. The foster mother apologized to Johnny for having left him, and she congratulated him on making the meal virtually on his own. She was impressed that he had been able to complete the task without her, and even without the aid of his distractible older sister. Likewise, she was amazed that Johnny had not expressed any disappointment in not receiving his weekly one-to-one time with her.

The next day the foster father went to the basement to clean up areas which had been neglected for months. After a few minutes, he yelled up from the basement, "Who cleaned off all the dust and dead insects from the window ledges?" It seemed to him incomprehensible that any of the children would have voluntarily cleaned up in the basement. When no one claimed to have cleaned up those window ledges, the foster parents began pondering the mystery.

It didn't take long for the foster mother to put two and two together. Johnny's seeming lack of anger after her absence the day before, the curious cleaning of the basement windows, and a slightly different taste and texture to the stew...Johnny had used a new ingredient in the family stew. He had fed them all insect parts and dust balls!

Vengeful behavior, as described above, derives from a sense the child has that it is safer to get even in indirect ways than to get mad in a direct fashion.

There is nothing as empowering as being a victim.

3. Feeling of Being a Victim

M any, if not most, troubled foster and adopted children have been victims. Physical, mental, sexual abuse, neglect, you name it, they've suffered through it. However accurate it is to describe these children as victims, we must not let them crystallize their role as victim. Many children hold onto that role and masochistically invite others to victimize them. Others, driven by insatiable needs for attention, waltz blithely and obliviously into sexually abusive encounters with perpetrators. Still others use their sad stories and gruesome tales of victimization to captivate others' sympathetic feelings.

Most problematic is the child who allows his sense of being a victim to justify a range of misbehavior. The justification may be: "Since I never get what I need from others, I steal." Or, "Since I was physically abused, I will take out my rage on the helpless others."

In dealing with children who feel chronically aggrieved and victimized, it is good to remember that there is nothing as empowering as being a victim. In this victim role, these troubled youngsters can rationalize all sorts of heinous, sadistic, and criminal behavior towards others. To these kids, it is always payback time.

(Some) children fail to learn from experience...it's like the joke about the man
with three penguins.

4. Inability to Profit from Experience

M any foster and adoptive parents report that their children fail to learn from experience. At school they forget by Tuesday what they learned on Monday. At home they can't master the routine, the family rules, or the overall rhythm of living with other human beings. Nor can they apply what they learned about not hurting the dog to not hurting the cat! To the foster or adoptive parents' frustration, each day the clock is reset. The child's counter goes back to zero. As one adoptive mother put it, "He's like Bill Murray in 'Groundhog's Day'...every day he has to learn the patterns all over again." It's like the joke about the man with the three penguins:

A car sped by a motorcycle cop hiding behind a billboard. The policeman caught up with the automobile - a convertible with its top down - and pulled the driver over. As he wrote a ticket and chastised the man for speeding, he was surprised to see three penguins sitting in the back seat. Handing the speeder his ticket, he told him to obey the law and he added, "Get those three penguins to the zoo where they belong!" Now, the next day the convertible sped by the parked motorcycle cop again. He caught up with the vehicle, and pulled it over a second time. Recognizing the car and the driver, the police officer angrily lit into the guy, writing him a citation. What made him even angrier was seeing the three penguins in the back seat with sunglasses. Lecturing the man on driving safety, the officer ended with, "And, I thought I told you yesterday to get those penguins back to the zoo." The driver innocently replied, "Well, yes officer, we had so much fun at the zoo, I thought I would take them to the beach today."

The inability to profit from experience - to retain, to generalize what is learned in one situation to the next, and to understand how what we do has consequences - concerns parents. And, it is no laughing matter for the child. With this inability comes a great deal of frustration on the part of both parent and child. The parents find themselves, in exasperated disbelief, reiterating rules, regulations and consequences that should by now be memorized and internalized by the child. The child's learning deficit often produces a parent who must constantly over-regulate, incessantly discipline, and perennially parent more negatively than he/she would like to. For the child, the inability to profit from experience brings frequent negative consequences and a sense of being unfairly treated by the world, along with a tendency to buck authority. Since the child has blurry recollections of prior learn-ing, yesterday's lessons, and even very recent consequences, he finds himself disci-plined and corrected, from his point of view, out of the clear blue sky. From his viewpoint, the outside world repeatedly blindsides him, punishing him for no good reason.

Shoplifting, "borrowing," and even full-blown kleptomania are common in children who come from backgrounds of maltreatment.

5. Stealing

*A*nnie was an eight-year-old girl recently placed in a residential treatment center for girls. Her birth parents were in prison for grand theft of an unusual sort. They stole lawn mowers. They stole landscaping equipment of all sorts. They even stole lawns! This creative couple found an outlet for their five-fingered sod and landscaping hardware via their own business, conveniently enough, in landscape architecture. After a spate of reports by other sod companies, the police dubbed the still unknown perpetrators Toro Terrorists. It was the case of "The Rapes of Grass."

Now Annie had her own idiosyncrasies and behavioral problems. Not surprisingly, after her parents were arrested, she was placed in three successive foster homes from which she ran away, trying to get back to her parents. In each of these homes she also lied and stole. Whatever she wanted she took and then sold or traded to others. She had learned to thieve and fence literally from professionals, e.g. her parents. Given her propensity to run, Annie was placed in a residential treatment center, where she could be watched around the clock by staff. Despite close supervision, she continued to steal and, what's more, one day she turned up missing. Annie was on the run, although the method was unique. She had stolen a riding lawn mower from the treatment center and driven off down a city street, turned left at the intersection and puttered down the entry ramp to the interstate highway. Her goal was to get to her parents. She was later apprehended in what the highway patrol called a low-speed chase.

Thievery in disturbed foster and adopted children is not always as unique as in this case. However, shoplifting, "borrowing," and even full-blown kleptomania are common in children who come from backgrounds of maltreatment.

Children with "learned chaos" can wreak havoc in their environment.

6. Chaotic Behavior

Chaotic, out-of-control, scattered behavior can simply exhaust the parents of troubled foster and adopted children. When asked to pin down what this symptom looks like at home, parents will often say, "It's not one thing...it's everything!" Children who are chaotic exude unfocused energy. They get into everything, they create a wake of turmoil, and they seem to thrive on chaos. Sometimes, behavior problems of this nature result in a diagnosis of Attention Deficit Hyperactivity Disorder or Bipolar Illness. In other instances, the behavior is clearly correlated to fetal alcohol syndrome or exposure in utero to drugs. With still other children, however, turmoil and anarchy were the hallmarks of their early lives. They were reared in upheaval and, as a result, have developed the condition called "learned chaos." The following illustration shows how some children with learned chaos can wreak havoc in their environment:

A foster mother I've know for years set an appointment to bring in a sibling group of three boys, ages 6, 4, and 3: Timmy, Tommy, and Teddy - the alliteration brothers. She mentioned that they were hyperactive.

When Mrs. Torgetsen arrived at the waiting room, I felt a slight tremor in the building. Was it an architectural response to the energy emanating from the three boys? Blessed with years of experience as a foster mother, Mrs. Torgetsen appeared to have adequate control over the boys at whom she glanced with a mixture of love and implied threat. That glance seemed to keep any gross misbehavior in check.

With the boys seated in their waiting room chairs, I asked the foster mother to accompany me to my office to fill me in on the boy's background, her observations of them, their current problems, etc. I wanted only ten minutes of her time alone before including the boys in the session. Mrs. Torgetsen gave me a look of doubt as she asked, "Will the boys be okay out here alone?" "Not to worry," I reassured her, "Selma, our receptionist, will be back from the Xerox room in a minute." With one more fixing stare at the boys, Mrs. Torgetsen accompanied me to my office down a long hallway.

Once seated, Mrs. Torgetsen blurted out with strained smile, "They've placed the Flying Wallendas with me!" "Why do you say that?" I laughed. "When they placed the boys with me two weeks ago, they waltzed in the front door as if they owned the place, and then they disappeared to explore. At first, I thought that it was just simple curiosity, but after ten minutes it seemed deathly quiet, so I went in search of them...I found all three of them doing a balancing act on the top railing of our balcony on the second floor! A death defying act!"

Just as she completed this story, there was a grating buzz on my intercom. Picking up, I somewhat testily asked Selma why the interruption in mid-session. In fact, I explained that she might hold her call to me except for dire emergencies. Selma politely but firmly responded, "You're term 'dire emergency' seems to fit a developing situation with these boys." Dropping the phone I raced the foster mother down the hall to the reception area. As we arrived in that room, we found ourselves splashing in a soggy shag carpet. The Flying Wallenda children had stopped up the sink next to the coffee maker and water had overflowed onto the floor, ponding on the waiting room carpet.

I should mention that I share an office with a psychologist who sees only adults. He can't relate to kids. His specialty is running assertiveness training groups for passive men, two of whom had shown up for their first group session. These two men sat in the corner of the room with their eyes wide open and alert and their knees drawn up to their chins, so as not to get their feet wet. They were dry but traumatized. Neither of these men had thought to go for help or to intervene with the kids. Only when Selma, our receptionist, returned belatedly to her post, had the adult world taken charge. I thought to myself, "These guys definitely need assertiveness training! But what would really toughen them up would be to place the Flying Wallenda children with them!"

When one "chaotic" child is placed with a foster or adoptive home, parenting becomes taxing. But, as in the case of the Flying Wallenda children (that is, the placement of multiple chaotic children) parenting challenges are endless.

7. Revolving Scapegoat Behavior

Revolving scapegoat behavior encompasses many problem behaviors which arise when there is a shift of children's roles within the foster or adoptive home. (Note: This frequently occurs when a sibling group has been placed with one family.) Usually a child who has historically assumed, or even invited, a scapegoat position in the family, begins to change for the better. As this child is observed by other children at home to receive more accolades and rewards for improved behavior, one or more of these observing children may abandon their present roles and take on the newly vacated scapegoat role. As foster and adoptive parents see it, when one child in the home gets better, inevitably one or more of the other youngsters get worse. As one child's problems decrease, another child develops problems. The children's unwritten rule seems to be: This family can only have one good child at a time.

When one child in the home gets better, inevitably one or more of the other youngsters get worse.

In analyzing this phenomenon, I don't believe it is a case of children consciously taking turns: "I'll be the bad child this week, and you assume that role next week." Nor is it a need on the family's part to have a scapegoat. (This was the assumption of family system's theory: namely, if one child after another emerges with problems, the family must need a problem child.) The most likely explanation is that formerly maltreated children frequently harken from homes where certain children enjoyed "favored nation's status," while their siblings experienced an emotional embargo. In other words, there were good children or bad children - stark categories. However, periodically, and sometimes unpredictably, the favored child might fall from grace or the scapegoat child might be temporarily forgiven, accepted, and treated better. When this happened the children learned to expect that a change in one of them meant changes for all. In foster and adoptive homes, this may explain why children seem to take turns in adopting the "bad" child role.

The poker face, the monosyllabic answers and the universal shrug of the shoulder seems aimed at dismissing the foster or adoptive parents.

8. Non-Communicativeness

There's nothing more frustrating than dealing with the child who won't talk. (Conversely, there's nothing quite as exhausting as the child who cannot stop communicating!) Some children will remain mute due to fearfulness or shyness. Or, they may not know what to say or how to say it. Others stay "mum" to keep out of trouble. They don't want to spill the beans. Still others defiantly button their lips and refuse to talk. They shut out adults completely, hopefully revealing nothing of how they feel, what they think, or where they have been. Case in point, the young teenager whose answer to every parental question is "I don't know."

Many disturbed foster and adopted children fall into this latter category. They show non-communicativeness in the extreme. Stonewall them with silence, is their wish. Keep the adult world at bay. Hide behind a sphinx-like facial mask and keep a stony silence. Maybe the adult world will just get tired of trying to communicate and go away!

While some non-communicativeness is the norm in teenagers, in some foster and adoptive children it underscores deep problems. These children interact little, hide most, and contribute nothing. They are resistant to the formation of an honest, reciprocal, give-and-take human relationship, especially with adults. The poker face, the monosyllabic answers and the universal shrug of the shoulder seem aimed at dismissing the foster or adoptive parents. To these youngsters it is simply safest to remain mute.

*Many (troubled children) are infants in big bodies, or babies
in oversized clothes.*

9. Emotional Immaturity

Many troubled foster and adopted children are psychologically stunted and emotionally immature. The needs which should have been met at younger ages were neglected, and these youngsters cannot move forward emotionally. This leaves tremendous discrepancies between physical size, chronological age, and emotional development. Many are infants in big bodies, or babies in oversized clothes. (Taylor & Wendelbo, 1997.)

Emotional immaturity is easier to understand than it is to remember. That is, most foster and adoptive parents can understand that the child's history of maltreatment or neglect has left psychological scars. And, they can easily grasp that the child has catching up to do. However, when it comes to the day-to-day parenting of a sizeable child, it is often difficult to remember that inside they are puny and emotionally delayed. The child's actual age and size delude us into forgetting remarkable delays. As a result, we can find ourselves relating based upon what we see rather than what we know about the child.

We should dose out our love, attention and worldly goods in amounts that can be swallowed and digested by the child.

10. Sense of Entitlement

When many children enter foster or adoptive families they experience sudden vertical mobility which catapults them out of past physical and emotional deprivation into the land of plenty, relatively speaking. Although we might expect that the change from certain forms of poverty, both physical and psychological, to plenitude would be a boon to their existence - it's not always that simple.

In the child's mind, growing up in a neglectful, emotionally impoverished home forms an expectation that children receive nothing, or very little, from caretakers. Thus, you better watch out for yourself if you are to survive. Take what you can, when you can, from whomever you can. With this dog-eat-dog mentality, the child may enter the foster or adoptive home to find that there are ample supplies, food, goods, possessions, and, oddly enough, parental attention. Although this is foreign to the child, he adapts - but occasionally not in the way we might hope. Our hope as adults is that the child will take from our horn of plenty and be satisfied, relaxed, reassured, and normalized. However, our hopes may be dashed, because many children add a layer of dysfunctional thought on top of their already jaded expectation. If goods are lavished upon them, a sense of bottomless, crass materialism builds upon their deeply entrenched negative expectations. Therefore, now they take what they can get - when they can, from whomever they can - and they feel entitled to it. We have, then, a formerly neglected child who not only feels a certain anger about having not received earlier in life, but now has the feeling that he deserves that horn of plenty.

Of course, children coming from impoverishment and neglect should be given tremendous amounts of good parenting. In most instances, they will flourish when receiving the physical and emotional bounty they had previously lacked. However, in some cases judicious generosity is in order. That is, we must be prudent about how we give to the child. Analogous to how the starving man is fed gradually back to normal weight, we should dose out our love, attention, and worldly goods in amounts that can be swallowed and digested by the child.

Family phobic children can become quite adept at terminating good foster or adoptive placements.

11. Family Phobia

Many foster and adoptive children cannot stand the intimacy and attachments found in family life. Ironically, they cannot accept what they need most, due to a deep fear of growing close to others. The reasons for this vary. Some children, raised for a good portion of their life in a residential setting or group home, may be classically institutionalized. They are more at home in the more impersonal, highly structured, and heavily populated world of a psychiatric hospital, a state institution, or a large treatment facility. Indeed, many of these children thrive in these settings prior to their move to a foster or adoptive home, only to self-destruct after placement in the family environment.

Other children, raised by a multitude of care-givers and traumatized by foster care drift, expect no family will be the last family - the permanent resting place of their wandering heart. Awaiting the inevitable demise of each home they enter, they derive some unholy satisfaction from expediting the end of the placement. Their motto: "Stop me, before I love again!"

A third group of children have been so maltreated by parent figures in their past they predict that any and all foster or adoptive parents will similarly abuse them. To them, trust of the adult is anathema. These children do not give new parent figures a chance to prove them wrong about all parents.

In any case, family phobic children can become quite adept at terminating good foster or adoptive home placements. Sabotaging family life and ending placements reduces the child's anxiety about intimacy and perhaps offers him some unusual sense of control of destiny.

12. Lying

Lying is an almost universal problem shown by troubled foster and adopted children. Frequently the companion to stealing, it provides the cover up, the excuse. At other times lying is more than that. It may be the reflexive, prevaricating answer to every question, no matter how innocuous.

Lying can be particularly troubling for foster and adoptive parents who cannot trust what the child tells them. Oftentimes, the child becomes so adept that he can mislead all but the most alert parent and professional. In some instances the child's falsehoods are so convincing and/or convoluted, that the child himself cannot decipher fact from fiction. Indeed, some children truly believe their own lies, which often makes them even more accomplished and convincing liars.

13. Self-Parenting Behavior

These comments come from care-givers of self-parented children, e.g. those who raised themselves:

"I feel completely unneeded," reported one discouraged foster mother.
"This child doesn't give me a chance to be his mother!" responded a deflated adoptive mother.
"We are totally superfluous. He never turns to us when sick, hungry or afraid. It's like he is avoiding us entirely," contended another adoptive couple.

Those foster and adopted children who simply refuse to be parented are very resistant to any interventions from parent figures whatsoever. Sadly, they do not leave openings for bonding, since they take care of all of their own needs, often solitarily. They studiously avoid any connections to their foster or adoptive parents. These children refuse to surrender to rules, direction, and guidance or to accept the love and affection the parents offer.

Some reasons for this "self-parenting" behavior follow:

      1. These children may have unresolved loyalty issues to birth parents;

      2. They raised themselves;

      3. They have lost too many care-givers in the past; or

      4. A combination of the above reasons.

Whatever the cause, self-parenting behavior totally exasperates many foster and adoptive parents who find themselves subtracted from the parenting equation. Without change in this problem behavior, discouraged parents feel like a big zero with the child and eventually stop trying to reach him/her.

14. Loss Sensitivity

Children who have experienced tremendous upheaval, abandonment and rejection grow sensitive to situations which connote loss: loss of attention, loss of position in a family, etc. External events such as parental illness, the birth of a child, the arrival of a new foster/adoptive child in the home, or a respite break by the parents may trigger a sense of loss. Internal events such as the shifts in the psychological intensity of a relationship or in the level of commitment from parents can also precipitate loss sensitivity, as in the following case:

Maggie, age nine-and-a-half, had resumed bed-wetting around the house. This problem was thought to be "solved" three years before. Why was Maggie wetting again? Why was she wetting secretly around the home? What had triggered the regression?

The facts of the case are that Maggie had lived with the Jones' foster family for five years. She had grown extremely attached to this family and considered them to be her "real" family. Typically, she did not want to have visits with her birth father.

Maggie's younger sister, Vanna (age six) was also placed with the Jones, although she remained in the care of her birth father until the previous year. Vanna looked forward to visits with her birth father and fantasized about reunions with him. She was showing no problems in the placement.

The birth father, Mr. Miller, remarried this year, a woman with her own two young sons. Mr. Miller has a history of suicidal depression with a seasonal component to it. He attempted suicide in front of Maggie and Vanna on one occasion. He has been frequently and regularly hospitalized, usually during the winter.

During a recent home visit with her father, Maggie was defiant, oppositional and mouthy during several confrontations with him. This was the first time she had acted this obstreperously with him.

In a recent hearing, Mr. Miller lost in his twelfth attempt to win back custody of Maggie and Vanna. After that hearing he seemed defeated and strangely accepting of the fact that Maggie and Vanna would remain in placement.

For their part, the foster parents had become exhausted by the never-ending series of court hearings regarding custody of the children. They had begun to talk more about "taking better care of ourselves," "taking time away from the kids," and "compassion burnout."

Several hypotheses swirl around this case:

1. Maggie's birth father had reinstituted hearings about custody several times. Maggie may be upset by the fact that she cannot live with her birth father. Conversely, she may worry that she might have to leave the foster family, where she has had good care.

2. Maggie may be reacting to her father's recent loss of the custody battle in court and to his apparent resignation to this fact.

3. Maggie may be reacting to the foster parents' exhaustion and compassion fatigue. The foster parents may have become depleted emotionally and may have subtly pulled back their emotional availability to Maggie.

It is highly likely that Maggie's recent regression signals loss sensitivity and anger over subtle abandonment. She had picked up on shifts in emotional availability and commitment from her birth father and almost simultaneously from her foster parents. All the adults in her world had become emotionally spent by the struggle over custody. Her day time wetting could be in direct response to her unverbalized grief reaction.

TWO

Our Foster and Adoptive Families

The bumper sticker on the car ahead reads, "Save A Child—Become A Foster Parent!" The ad on TV pleads, "Consider another option...the Adoption Option!" Recruitment of foster and adoptive parents is on-going, and yet we cannot obtain and retain enough foster and adoptive parents to keep up.

Why don't we have enough homes for waiting children? Why do caseworkers desperately scramble to find a good home for each new foster child? Theories abound. We know that families in general are stressed financially and personally. The stay-at-home Mom (or Dad) is a vanishing breed. Financial incentives for doing foster care are inadequate, rarely covering the untold costs, and are less than minimum wage when broken down hourly. Adoptive parents are made aware that subsidies to pay for the children's extraordinary needs are approved on a year-to-year basis, with no real long-term guarantees.

Other theories center upon the growing awareness of prospective foster and adoptive parents concerning the magnitude of problems kids bring with them into the home. Also, there is the ubiquitous specter of false allegations of abuse against foster and foster/adoptive parents. Further, some foster and adoptive parents unbelievably find themselves incriminated and blamed for the very problems the children brought with them into care.

Theories aside, raising a troubled child, our modern day Cain, raises many issues for foster and adoptive parents, among which are the following:

1. Victimization of foster and adoptive mothers by the disturbed child.

2. Coping with the "least preferred child" and his undying fantasy of reuniting with his birth family.

3. Living a fish bowl existence which can inhibit good foster and adoptive parenting.

4. Discovery that other children are used as targets for the disturbed foster or adopted child.

5. Dealing with the occasional unhelpful, helping professionals.

6. Increased demands to collaborate with birth parents.

7. Awareness that subclinical problems in foster and adoptive parents may become full-blown difficulties under stress.

These seven important issues are discussed next.

Children who have loved and lost one or more mother figures accumulate a mass of feelings about "the mothering one".

1. Foster and Adoptive Mothers as Victims

It is almost inevitable that foster and adoptive children with histories of separation, loss and maltreatment develop "mother issues." Children who have loved and lost one or more mother figures accumulate a mass of feelings about "the mothering one." When there have been multiple losses or trauma related to mothers, youngsters accumulate a variety of potent feelings toward those who have, in the past, mothered them and toward those who, in the present, are attempting to mother them.

The feelings which troubled foster and adopted children have collected regarding mothers are numerous, contradictory and convoluted. On the one hand these children may have positive, often times, over-idealized and Polly-annish feelings toward mothers. On the other hand, youngsters may have rage-filled emotions attached to mothers. Some children who have experienced many mother figures have specific, clear recollections toward past mothers; however, others may have vague, nonspecific, and blurred memories. Especially where children have had numerous, nameless caretakers in an orphanage setting or when they had a plethora of relatives, strangers, and/or foster parents in rapid succession, they often cannot differentiate one mother figure from the next.

Foster and adoptive mothers often fall victim to feelings about mothers that the child has collected over time. Not uncommonly, these new mothers inherit negative, or at the least ambivalent, emotions derived from the child's past life with mothers. In a typical placement, the child may project only a few of his/her many emotions at the present foster or adoptive mother. On occasion, the child may direct the full range of collected feelings and expectations toward her. For instance, the child may direct tremendous hate, rejection and venom toward the foster mother (who is an undeserving target), while he holds his birth mother or past foster or adoptive mothers in a reverential position. Similarly, the child may allow himself to feel extremely warm feelings toward a female (or male) therapist, teacher or other adult, while rejecting his foster or adoptive mother.

(Therapists, myself included, are often tempted to form overly close bonds with children who project the warm, positive, over-idealized image and feelings of mother onto us. Unfortunately, rather than encouraging the child to cease his resistance toward the foster or adoptive parents, we may inadvertently promote the over-idealized fantasy that the child holds toward us. This may result in an undermining of the relationship to the foster or adoptive mother.)

Attached to a fantasy, many youngsters pin their hopes on an ephemeral star and wager on the long shot.

2. Coping with the Least Favored Child

Commonly, youngsters who received appallingly inadequate parenting, after placement in the foster or adoptive home, hold on longest to the three D's: denial, displacement, and dreaming. These children deny their feelings of disappointment with birth parents. Their unverbalized anger is displaced onto undeserving foster or adoptive parents. They dream unrelentingly about reuniting with those who have sometimes given them next to nothing. (Ironically, when these children have been least preferred and sometimes unwanted, they tenaciously ward off families who do want them, e.g. foster and adoptive parents.) This denial, displacement and dreaming trio challenges the foster and adoptive parents' coping capacities, since the unrelenting message from the child is to punish or reject them. It is the rare parent who can perennially receive such negative messages and cope effectively with the task of raising the child. Siblings, who received better care and who were given adequate or even preferential treatment in their family of origin, often let go and move on, psychologically speaking. One might expect the opposite, e.g. that children who were least favored in their family of origin would have fewer loyalty issues and related barriers to blending into a new home, while the favored, preferred youngsters, would hold onto allegiances which might prevent incorporation into a new family. However, it is the children who received the smallest amounts of parental attention and love, children who were passed over or unwanted, children who were the least favored, that often cling most tenaciously to their past, attached to a fantasy. Many youngsters pin their hopes on an ephemeral star and wager on the long shot, as we see next.

Paul, a fifteen-year-old, middle of three children, was placed with his younger sister (age 10) in an experienced foster family. Although all of the children had been neglected, Paul was the mother's least favorite offspring. He had been the most frequent recipient of physical abuse, and the victim of heinous sexual abuse by his birth mother's boyfriend.

The foster mother mentioned three central concerns about Paul. First, he was phoney and unnaturally pleasant with her. Secondly, he fantasized incessantly about returning to his birth mother, although she had abandoned the children two years before and her whereabouts were unknown. Finally, he seemed fanatically preoccupied with getting his sister in trouble.

Paul's constellation of problems is common among children who have been the least favorite, most neglected, generally unwanted children in families of origin. The phony, unreal pleasantness often accompanied by a saccharin, fawning, ingratiating approach inevitably grates against those who live with the child. Foster and adoptive mothers frequently complain that they cannot find the real child, cannot get to the true feelings, and cannot stand the artificial relationship to this youngster. "Give me a child who shows a little (or even a lot) of anger or true emotion and I can work with him...but, this fakery drives me nuts." In many cases this seemingly innocuous pleasantness can be the undoing of the placement. Simply put, mothers find it exasperating to deal with the sham. Beyond that, there is an absence of real emotion, especially real anger and genuine affection, from the foster/adopted child. Foster or adoptive mothers (and sometimes fathers) discover a responding depth of anger in themselves which is unsettling. In effect, they feel and sometimes express the child's submerged feelings. These submerged feelings often include voluminous rage at mother figures who are viewed as neglectful, rejecting, and unfair distributors of maternal love. The child is often unaware of these negative sentiments which have arisen in the unfulfilling relationship to the birth mother, who is staunchly idealized. (In Chapter 4 we will describe the strategy entitled "Pledge of Allegiance" which focuses upon these submerged feelings, the 3 D's, and how one foster mother coped with the child's routine dismissal of her.)

The foster mother's third concern about Paul, e.g. his preoccupation with getting his sister in trouble, in some ways was the most problematic, disconcerting, and destabilizing of the placement. Paul's compulsion to tattle, instigate disruptions, and set his sister up was baffling and maddening. When he would provoke her to anger he often smiled as she exploded and then was accordingly punished for her misbehavior. His torment of his sister was continual, but heightened after he witnessed her getting positive parental attention. This seemed to fuel a burning jealousy and to confirm his sense of himself as the least preferred, overlooked, etc.

3. Fish Bowl Existence

We wonder why foster and adoptive parents disappear after their home studies have been completed. But, after being interviewed, screened, fingerprinted, investigated, psychoanalyzed and otherwise placed under the microscope, it's no surprise they'd like to get back to what they do best, e.g. parenting. Additionally, foster and adoptive parents in the fish bowl may be reluctant to report difficulties with the children who have finally been placed with them for fear of appearing uncommitted, incompetent, or even trouble-making.

Foster and adoptive parents in the fish bowl may be reluctant to report difficulties with the children who have finally been placed with them.

Indeed, it is normal for foster and adoptive parents to "take the baby and run" as far away from professional services as possible, as soon as feasible (Delaney and Kunstal, 1993). Unfortunately, especially in the case of special needs adoptions, this disappearing act can prevent the provision of supports to the parents which could ultimately prevent or reduce problems which emerge with the troubled child.

Although we attempt to prepare these parents for the challenges ahead, it is not until the foster or adoptive parents have lived with the children for a time that they may truly understand what they are in for. Sadly, away from the fish bowl existence at last, they may not return for help until very near the end.

Essentially, it is quite understandable why foster and adoptive parents often retreat from help. However, without help many placements can become irretrievably broken. Ultimately, retreat may result in defeat and disruption of the placement.

The hazards of being one of the other children in the foster or adoptive home range widely.

4. Other Children as Targets in the Foster or Adoptive Home

Raising troubled foster or adoptive children may be hazardous to the health of other children in the home: other less disturbed foster or adoptive children, younger birth children, visiting grandkids, and the like. These children, figuratively speaking, play Abel to the disturbed child's role of Cain.

The hazards of being one of the other children in the foster or adoptive home range widely. Time and attention from foster or adoptive parents become steadily less. When a needy child enters the family scene, for instance, a shift in parental effort and focus upsets the equilibrium. Further, when the needs of this arriving child are all-consuming, other children are left emotionally short-changed. There's only twenty-four hours in a day and the neediest child wants them all. In homes where needy foster or adopted children consumed the lion's share of parental time, other children may develop problems to redirect the focus to themselves.

Beyond time allocation issues, there is the issue of overt victimization of other children by the disturbed foster or adoptive child. Threats, physical assaults, manipulation, seduction, and coercion crop up, sometimes unbeknownst to the parents. Children may be groomed for sexual exploitation or set up as the patsy in other schemes without the parents knowing. It can be quite dangerous being a child in a home with a troubled foster or adoptive child.

Jamie had inflicted pain upon his siblings, his foster father and on himself - he needed to understand that!

5. Dealing with Unhelpful, Helping Professionals

Unfortunately, some foster and adoptive parents occasionally encounter individual helping professionals who may inadvertently do more harm than good. When helping professionals lack knowledge or experience concerning the special areas of foster and adoptive care, they may provide unhelpful advice and consultation. In addition, they may grossly misperceive the needs of the child and the family, as in the following case:

In the adoption of three brothers, the prospective single parent dad had fostered the trio for almost two years when he was faced with an excruciating decision. The middle boy, Jamie, was too disturbed for him to handle. Despite psychotherapy two times weekly, this boy continued to fire-set. Jamie was violent toward the youngest brother and seemed insanely jealous of any attention paid to his two brothers by the foster/ adoptive dad. The problem was compounded by the fact that Jamie was the child victimized most severely by his biological father, who favored him and targeted him simultaneously. Jamie had a "trauma bond" to his perpetrator and wished to reunite with him. However, his birth father was in prison for twenty years with no early release. This left Jamie with extremely ambivalent feelings about adoption. He was constantly undermining incorporation into the family, all the while demanding attention, most of it negative.

Rather than jeopardizing the placement of the other two boys, the adoptive father suspected that Jamie would have to be moved. After watching the adoptive father struggled with guilt and indecision for a good six months, the caseworker stepped in and decided for him. A termination session was scheduled in the therapist's office. The adoptive father, remorseful about "failing" this son, took on all of the blame for the disruption of his home. "It was me...all me," was the father's theme in the session. Unfortunately, the therapist and caseworker allowed him to take the blame. In fact, when Jamie voiced that he had a part in the demise of the placement, they rushed in to absolve him of all blame in the matter saying, "You are just a child." Jamie had inflicted pain upon his siblings, his foster father and on himself - he needed to understand that!

As the above case illustrates, the tendency to alleviate pain in the child prevented the well-intended therapist and caseworker from helping the child profit from his loss of this family. Jamie's rudimentary insight into his role in the placement disruption should have been nurtured not quashed. At the same time, the adoptive father should not have been saddled with the onus of the placement failure. After all, this man had attempted the next to impossible in adopting a large, disturbed sibling group. He has to carry on with the two other boys in as strong a way as possible. We do not want the adoptive father endlessly struggling with his misplaced guilt over Jamie.

Many foster parents find birth family involvement taxing even when it is limited to visitation, which in itself can gravely disrupt the child.

6. Increased Demands to Collaborate with Birth Parents

The trend across the United States is to ask more from foster parents and foster/ adoptive parents than ever before. In one area, specifically - working together with the birth parents of the foster/adoptive children - we may at times ask too much. Foster parents are asked to mentor and train, to supervise visits, as well as to act as respite homes for birth parents.

While hypothetically it makes sense to use foster parent expertise to support struggling birth parents, it is certainly yeoman's work. Indeed, the reaction of many foster parents to this notion is, "This is too much to ask." Traditionally, foster parents have been entrusted with the protection and care of children, not with engaging their parents. A good many foster parents understandably balk at collaborating with biological family members who have mistreated the children now in foster care. Many foster parents find birth family involvement taxing even when it is limited to visitation, which in itself can gravely disrupt the child.

The term "shared parenting" has been applied to the process of cooperative partnerships of foster and birth parents (Steinhauer, 1991). Maluccio (1992) sees this as the wave of the future in family foster care. However, I am convinced that most foster parents will not accept the role of birth family supporter very eagerly. Especially not in cases where they feel that the birth parents are threatening, invasive, and/or untreatable. Coercing foster parents to collaborate in those situations might seriously jeopardize the child's placement, and may needlessly drive the foster family out of foster care work.

The mother seemed icy cold and withdrawn from this girl.

7. Subclinical Problems in Foster and Adoptive Parents: The Case of the Princess and the Pauper

As might be expected, some foster and adoptive parents experience personal problems, psychological difficulties, and even psychiatric disorders which interfere with or preclude successful parenting of troubled foster and adopted children. Some of these problems only become manifestly evident after the placement of the troubled child, as in the following:

Two adopted sisters, now 12 and 14, had been with their foster/adoptive parents for nine years. The couple sought mental health services when these girls became severely rivalrous and competitive toward each other and incessantly demanding of parental attention.

The therapist observed that the adoptive mother was symbiotically enmeshed with the younger adopted girl, who she treated preferentially. By contrast, the older daughter clashed with the mother constantly. The mother seemed icy cold and withdrawn from this girl. She was consistently hostile, and sometimes cruel, toward her younger sister, whom she called derisively, "The Little Princess."

The adoptive father was aware of the inequitable treatment his wife displayed toward the girls. While passive and non-confronting toward his wife, he attempted to compensate, to counterbalance. He walked a tightrope, as he tried to remain loyal to all three females in his life.

Individual psychotherapy with the girls was attempted at first. However, the jealousy and animosity between them persisted undeterred. Several issues are germane to this case:

(1) The older girl was more troubled when she initially arrived in the adoptive home. She had lived in physical squalor and emotional dysfunction much longer than her younger sister. Additionally, when first placed, she had remained staunchly attached to her birth mother's memory and immediately rejected the adoptive mother. This prompted the adoptive mother to recoil and to reach out to the other child almost defensively.

(2) The adoptive mother had enjoyed a symbiotic, hostile-dependent bond to her own mother, who was an overly controlling, needy matriarch. The adoptive mother's older sister was clearly preferred by the mother, but had died in a car wreck in her early twenties. Interestingly, the older sister's death ten years ago was a contributing factor to the initiation of the adoption process. While some of these historic family conflicts had emerged in the adoptive home study a decade earlier, the depth of the past problem appeared only years after the adoption.

(3) The adoptive mother seemed to project her "bad self" onto her older daughter. She, in some ways, associated her with her older sister who had maintained, until her untimely death, in the preferred child role. In effect she "pauperized" her older daughter, recoiling from her and neglecting her emotional needs. Additionally, the adoptive mother projected her "ideal self" onto her younger adopted daughter, with whom she could have the enmeshed relationship she never had with her own mother.

Parents need help in raising children to new heights.

THREE

Family-Based Strategies for Helping Troubled Youngsters

Simply put, foster and adoptive parents need direction in devising helpful strategies which can be employed with their troubled youngsters. Parents need help in raising children to new heights. Caseworkers, therapists, as well as foster/adoptive parent support groups, can assist the individual foster or adoptive family to address the serious problems of their youngsters.

In this chapter we set out an approach for looking at solutions for children's problems. In this approach we look beyond the surface problem to its underlying meaning for the child. Instead of addressing symptoms alone, we search out the genesis of the problems. Additionally, we focus on side-stepping power struggles with the child while harnessing the child's negative energy to propel him in the direction of healthier functioning. Specifically, we next turn to discussions of the following:

1. A new model for delivering mental health services.

2. Interpreting the underlying meaning of behavior problems.

3. Questions which guide strategy building.

1. A New Model for Delivery of Mental Health Services

When it comes to troubled foster and adoptive care, the core of treatment is the family milieu, parallel to the therapeutic milieu of the residential treatment center. The mental health professional (caseworkers and teachers) stand in important supportive and consultative positions to the family.

Therapists and other helping professionals must aim for the stabilizing of placements and the maximizing of the family's inherent healing process. They must employ a consultative and catalytic function - helping the family in its therapeutic role with the child. While contributing expertise, the mental health professional must shun the role of "expert," assisting the family to build on its own intrinsic and growing expertise.

Some guidelines for working effectively with families include the following:

a. Meet with parents in order to understand their perceptions and insights about the child.

b. Include parents in most, if not all, sessions.

c. Be judicious of indirect, one-to-one psychotherapy with the child.

d. Re-examine the issue of confidentiality in terms of the new view of the foster and adoptive parents as team members.

e. Be alert to opportunities to assist the family in confrontation of problem behavior, manipulation and deception by the child.

f. Become concerned if the child seems to enjoy the psychotherapy sessions, while failing to improve in the home.

g. Do not place self in the "idealized parent" role with the child.

Brief, intermittent, long-term psychotherapy (BILT-P):

A new framework for mental health services to children in out-of-home care engages children over a substantial period of time, with concerted effort during predictable periods of crisis and transition (e.g. when potential for positive change may be at its zenith).

BILT-P, or brief, intermittent, long-term psychotherapy, describes in its title the gist of how mental health services are delivered to the child (and foster family):

> • Each individual series of interventions are circumscribed: six to ten sessions.
> • The needs or problem areas are objectified and baseline measures taken at the onset.
> • A treatment plan is sculpted to address the needs and problems and intervention would start.
> • At the end of the first series of 6 to 10 sessions, an assessment (or post-test) is conducted to see how the child was progressing. In many instances it might be found that adequate gains had been made. Changes in the child and in the character of the placement would be sufficient to suspend active involvement in therapy for the time being.

Intermittency of the psychotherapy speaks to the necessity for periodic treatment with troubled foster children. Many will need brief treatment at the onset of placement to help with incorporation into the foster family, with grief over loss of the birth family, and with issues surfacing in visitation with birth parents. Then, later a series of interventions may be fitting when the child deals with issues around a failure to return home to birth family in a timely fashion. Very predictably, the child will require intervention when and if he is moving toward return to the birth family or when he is being prepared to live with kin or a prospective adoptive home.

Long-term implies that for many, one-shot, brief psychotherapy cannot realistically address the serious, potentially disruptive problems which emerge in placement over time - especially with more troubled youngsters. When a foster child is in placement for six months or longer, brief interventions may span the entire length of stay. In treating a seriously troubled, adopted child, psychotherapy may be employed almost continuously, with only rare interruptions.

The Use of "Invisible Therapies" for Youngsters in Placement:

Traditionally, when we think about psychotherapy for children, conventional approaches come to mind: play therapy, behavior modification, and family therapy. We recall the trips to the mental health clinic, the wait in the reception area, and the confidential confessional the child enters for his/her "fifty minute hour." In this traditional model of mental health, the expert (the central change agent) and therapist are one and the same: the mental health professional.

As controversial as it sounds, traditional therapy is often times not a good match for children who live in foster homes, group facilities, special needs adoptive placements, and/or residential care. Indeed, in the worst case scenario, conventional psychotherapy may inadvertently undermine the stability of placements. At the least, orthodox psychotherapy may have little or no relevance to; 1) stabilizing the child's life while in placement; 2) confronting acting-out behaviors which threaten the continuity of placement, or 3) addressing relationship issues in placement which are at the core of the child's progress.

The concept of "invisible therapies" (as described by one Canadian foster care program), endorses the belief that the foster or placement family is **the** expert (**the** central change agents) and **the** true therapists to children in their care. Foster parents, legal risk foster/adoptive parents, group home parents, and special needs adoptive parents are lead members of the therapy team. Rather than being relegated to waiting in the reception area of a mental health clinic, these parents are actively included in therapy sessions. Issues arising in their homes with their children become important grist for the therapeutic mill. Strategies for managing the child's acting-out behavior, for fostering better verbalization of emotion, for engendering negotiation and social skills, and for promoting positive relationships and healthier attachments to others are developed by the therapy teams (composed of agency worker, foster or adoptive parents, mental health counselor, and others, as needed).

Invisible therapy is ubiquitous in foster and adoptive placements. The child's unvarnished emotion, habitual misbehaviors, cynical misperceptions of intimacy, and un-relenting problems with attachment formation, all emerge in full force. The potency of emotion which arises in family settings is unparalleled, and correctly channeled, allows for maximum gains by the child. Consultation with the therapy team allows the parents to apply invisible therapy to the child. Consistency and surprise, directness and paradox, and most fundamentally, the relationships which foster and adoptive parents supply, comprise the invisible therapy provided for children.

2. Interpreting the Underlying Meaning of Behavior Problems

In working with troubled foster and adopted children, many professionals employ behavior modification to address problem areas. If the child acts out, there are punishments. If the child inhibits acting out, there are rewards. While behavior modification has great efficacy in some work with children, with troubled foster or adopted children it often falls short. Indeed, such interventions with children are susceptible to failure, "symptom substitution," or only temporary success when we fail to take into account the driving forces behind, and the underlying meaning of, the behavior problems.

Foster and adoptive parents, caseworkers, and therapists are often puzzled by inexplicable, unfathomable behavior problems in their charges. Their puzzlement is natural and often leads to better understanding of the child, especially if they focus on this question: What does the behavior problem communicate about unspoken conflicts, needs, and/or feelings of the child?

In the following case illustration, one teenager's behavior spoke volumes about her unspoken feelings:

Debbie, a fifteen-year-old foster girl, had lived in a treatment foster home for 18 months. She had made substantial gains in controlling her behavior at home and in achieving school grades which the caseworker had thought impossible at the time of placement. Control battles and passive aggressive behaviors - the core of many of her home and school problems - had materially subsided. Plans were underway to attempt family reunification, placing the child back with her family of origin. Only one barrier remained. This young lady stubbornly clung to one last problem, i.e. she refused to change her underwear and had thwarted all attempts to resolve this hygiene issue which had aggravated her birth parents for years. In the past, rewards for hygienic behavior or punishment for non-hygienic behavior had produced no improvements. But, we may ask, "why not?"

The therapist speculated that it was Debbie's last vestige of control and that having surrendered all other battles, this final battleground remained. Further, this hygiene issue symbolized some resistance to total compliance and loss of her old role as one who fought against anything smacking of adult control.

When Debbie was confronted with the reality that this unappealing, latest behavior problem stood in the way of her return to her biological family, she vocalized her desire to live with her birth mother and father. Though she ostensibly desired reunion with her family, questions were wisely raised by the foster parents who suspected ambivalent feelings on the part of both Debbie and her birth parents. The birth parents, though verbalizing support of the notion of Debbie's return, consistently failed to increase the frequency and duration of home visits. In fact, some visits were shortened, canceled, or even overlooked.

Debbie's acting-out behavior most likely stemmed from her own ambivalence about returning home and from her unverbalized sense of her birth parents' wavering commitment to her planned return. This new understanding of Debbie's acting-out behavior will conceivably help in designing useful interventions. For instance, re-defining this case as a long-term foster placement, rather than a family reunification case, might reduce acting-out dramatically.

In another case illustration, a younger child's acting-out raised speculation about an underlying meaning to the problem. Correctly interpreting the misbehavior, and correspondingly devising appropriate interventions, could lead to reduction of acting-out, as seen next:

Hank, an eight-year-old foster/adopted boy had lived with his present family for three years as a foster child. After the first year his frequently stated desire was to be adopted by this family. However, simultaneously he developed problems, wetting his bed at night regularly for the first time in two years. He began to perpetrate sexually against one of the previously adopted children in the home, and to fight bitterly with other children in the home. What had gone wrong? Why the resurgence in acting-out? Why had this all returned now? What triggered this downturn?

In my initial meeting with the foster/adoptive mother, she revealed that the onset of acting-out occurred three months prior. It was at that time when the boy had been told that he was free for adoption and that his dream of adoption would become a reality. He seemed immediately pleased, but shortly thereafter he began to look distant and preoccupied, and then came the problem behaviors. Was he really wanting to be adopted after all? Had talk of the adoption awakened loyalty issues toward his birth mother? (Certainly this would be one avenue to explore with him. However, it appeared that he had no obvious remaining allegiance to his birth mother, and in fact had experienced no contact with her for four years. If allegiance to her was an issue, it must be deeply submerged. For purposes of helping this boy, exploring a "reunion fantasy" might be a dead end.)

In probing further, we found that this boy's two siblings had been adopted by another family a year earlier, though they had been the last to be removed from the birth home. That is, Hank had been the first removed from the birth mother and the last to be adopted. What did his early removal say about the nature of his problematic relationship to his biological mother? What did it suggest about her preference for the other two children? What could this reveal about his status as an unwanted child in his family of origin? Additionally, what did the suspected issue of being a problematic, least preferred, and possibly unwanted child have to do with the recent acting out?

As if there weren't already enough possible factors to juggle, questions were raised about the placement history of the child. The child had experienced two prior foster home placements after removal from his birth family at the age of four. Further, he had one adoptive experience, admittedly brief, in which a family backed out before placement, but not until after two months of week-end visits which he enjoyed. Were multiple past placements related to the recent acting out? Had those past placements raised serious doubts in this boy? Had Hank's hopes been dashed to the ground by the aborted adoption, rendering adoption a frightening, if tantalizing dream?

In the end, the most helpful hypothesis was that Hank reacted negatively to the bursting of a secret part of his adoption fantasy. With his quest to be adopted nearly at an end and with the announcement of the pending adoption, one might expect Hank to be most excited and pleased. However, the news of the finalization may have brought a painful awareness. Specifically, he was to be adopted into this family with all the children in the home. In fantasy, Hank may have dreamed of exclusive attention from an adoptive mom who would raise him as an only child, a preferred child, a wanted child.

Now, the truth be known, all the above described hypotheses are interesting but only worthwhile if they help us in the development of strategies which will reach this child, reduce his disruptive acting-out and ensure adoptive stability. In this instance, we need to focus on meeting Hank's need for exclusivity with the adoptive mom via uninterrupted, one-to-one time with her. (This would not be time earned by good behavior, but time which is supplied freely, non-contingently, in an attempt to reduce the anger over *sharing time and attention.) To specifically target the issues of bed-wetting, sexual acting-out, and bitter fighting might help to some extent. However, without strategies aimed directly at the need for exclusivity, we should not expect much change. While Hank will never be an only child in this home, by stepping-up individual time with his mother, we might reduce his disappointment enough to permit him to fit in, to share love, etc.*

In both case illustrations, positive change in the child's functioning will only occur when we identify and interpret the underlying meaning of behavior problems. With that, we have information which will improve the design of effective interventions with the child.

In the next section, we will move to the enumeration of questions which improve our understanding of the child and family and which enhance our therapeutic strategy building process.

Many parents seek a "guru" for answers. However, frequently we will find the best solutions, if we just ask the right questions.

3. Questions Which Guide Strategy Building

When a child is struggling in placement, it's not always easy to figure out what to do to help him. When foster or adoptive families have a disturbed child on their hands, they frequently run out of ideas. And the questions arise: What do we do next? Is there anything that we haven't tried? Can any approach ever reach this child? Can we even hang on? We've tried everything we know - so now what? It is at this point that many parents seek a "guru" for answers. However, frequently we will find the best solutions, if we just ask the right questions.

Often times the relationship of the foster or adoptive family to the child or vice versa grows so negative, we wonder if it can turn around. Further, all too often the child is getting to the parents, before the parents can reach the child. Can the foster or adoptive family stop marching to the beat of the child's drum and play a new tune that he'll dance to?

When children fail to respond to conventional, tried and true parenting approaches, standard forms of psychotherapy, and traditional family therapy, we may need to design strategies and interventions which go beyond the norm. Delaney (1996), Kunstal and Delaney (1993), and Fahlberg and Delaney (in press) describe unconventional family-based strategies which address difficult emotional and behavioral problems in foster and adoptive children. Often recommended in these books are interventions which side-step power struggles and overcome obstacles that stand in the way of reaching the disturbed youngster. Psychotherapists, caseworkers, and parents are advised to re-frame problems, to bend swords into plowshares, and to use innovative, caring approaches to help these troubled foster and adoptive children.

The following questions, grouped under six categories, cover issues important to the process of building strategies which may help the child and the family:

I. The Behavior Problems of the Child

A. What are the specific behavioral problems of the child?

B. What is the historical meaning of the behavior problem or symptom?
C. What is the need underlying the behavior?
D. What does the problem tell us about the child's emotional age or level of functioning?
E. In the past, how did the behavior problem allow the child to survive physically and/or emotionally in the family?
F. How does the behavior protect the child against attachment and loss?
G. Are the current problem behaviors the same or different from those in past placements?
H. Has the behavior improved or worsened over time?
I. How long has the child been in this placement? Was there a honeymoon?
J. Has the child experienced multiple care-givers, frequent separation and loss, and multiple foster and/or adoptive placements?
K. How severe is/are the behavior problem(s)?
L. What is the frequency of the problem?
M. Does the problem occur predictably or erratically?
N. Are there any obvious cycles or patterns associated with the behavior problems?
O. How controlling and oppositional is the child?

II. Relationship Variables

A. How does the child view family—this family—families in general?
B. What is the child's perceptions of mothers, fathers, siblings? Does the child relate differently to adult males versus adult females?
C. Does the foster or adoptive placement recapitulate significant factors in the child's earlier life?
D. Does the child play family members against each other? Is other splitting going on?
E. Has the child gone from "rags to riches," from emotional impoverishment to psychological entitlement?
F. If this is a sibling placement, do siblings play "revolving scapegoat" roles?

G. Does the child idealize the biological parents while denying anger toward them?

H. Is the child drawn to strangers while shunning available attachment figures?

I. How have the dynamics shifted within the foster or adoptive home since the child entered the picture?

J. Do family members view the child and the child's behavior differently? In what ways? How do family members feel about the child? Have family members established feelings of attachment for this child?

K. Can the child accept affection/touch and positive feedback from others?

L. What is the child's response to visitation with relatives?

M. How does the child respond to respite care?

N. Does the child have attachments? What type?

III. Other Underpinnings of the Behavioral Problems

A. How much abuse of the child occurred before the child was verbal?

B. Does the child have physical, medical, developmental, cognitive, and/or psychiatric problems which relate to the behavioral problems?

C. Has the child suffered neurological insult related to his or her behavior problems?

D. Do temperamental and genetic issues explain any of the behavior problems?

E. Has the child taken medication for his/her emotional/behavioral problems? What has the response been to each?

IV. Triggers to Loss Sensitivity

A. Has a new child moved into the foster or adoptive home?

B. Has there been a birth of a child in the placement?

C. Do the foster or adoptive parents have present health problems?

D. How does the child react to respite care or vacations by the foster or adoptive parents?

E. Is the child beginning to feel attached, to develop a sense of belonging in the foster or adoptive home?

F. Has the child reacted positively, negatively, or with ambivalence toward the finalization of the adoption?

G. How does the child respond to canceled, missed, shortened, or disappointing visits with birth family members?

H. Does the child seem to respond to court dates and/or to the foster or adoptive parents feelings of trepidation about court dates?

I. With the onset of preadolescence or adolescence, how has the child reacted to the dependence-independence dilemma (e.g. the desire to remain forever dependent versus the drive to become self-sufficient.)?

J. Has a child been recently moved out of the foster or adoptive home?

K. Is the child aware of any sickness, death, or other crises or significant changes in the lives of his birth relatives?

L. What anniversary reactions underlie the child's current behavior problems?

V. Echoes from the Past of the Foster or Adoptive Parents

A. What is the nature of the attachment relationships of the foster or adoptive parents and their own parents?

B. Have the foster or adoptive parents experienced significant losses, e.g. suicide of a sibling, death of a parent, disappearance of a child, SIDS, loss of other foster or adoptive child, etc.?

C. Is the foster or adoptive parent a survivor of sexual or physical abuse?

D. What is the nature of foster or adoptive parents to their own siblings?

E. Is the foster or adoptive child's behavior resurrecting unresolved developmental issues of the parent?

F. Have the adoptive parents resolved infertility issues?

VI. Miscellaneous Factors Related to the Behavior Problems

A. What has helped to reduce or eliminate the problems?

B. What has failed to help or has made the problems worse?

C. How does the child display anger?

D. Does the child demand exclusive attention?

E. Has the child sufficiently grieved the loss of past relationships?

F. Does the child harbor fantasies of reunion with birth relatives?

G. Does the child generally benefit from systematic reinforcement or does he manipulate and exploit behavior reinforcement, token economy plans, and level systems?

H. Does the child respond negatively to success, improvement, and increasing feelings of belonging to a family?

I. What is the child's present diagnosis? What other diagnostic labels have been given in the past?

J. How does the child react to rewards, token economy, behavior modification, and structure?

K. Do most interventions only remain successful for a short period of time?

L. Does the child have strengths which can be promoted?

M. Is the family open to using unconventional strategies?

Note: When developing any interventions there needs to be protection in place to guard against misuse of strategies, harm to the child, as well as insensitivities to the child's history, developmental age, past trauma, etc. The interventions should, of course, be legal, abide by state regulations, and be in the child's best interests. One of the best protections of safety comes in the use of a multi-disciplinary team (e.g. the therapist, social worker, and parents) which develops and sanctions the interventions jointly with its members.

In all cases, the objective of development of intervention should take into account the child's health and well-being, the need for placement stability, the reduction of stress upon the host family, and the healthy empowerment of the foster or adoptive parents. Overall treatment goals are described elsewhere (see Kunstal and Delaney [1993], and Delaney [1991]), but should focus upon: containing acting-out behavior; increasing verbalization of emotion; improving negotiation skills, and increasing positive encounters between the child and family.

Specific stategies are needed when children's misbehavior ties up all parental energies.

FOUR

Sample Strategies

We turn now to sixteen sample strategies developed by foster or adoptive parents - in concert with their caseworker, therapist, and/or their parent support/staffing group - which address behavioral problems of their children. Specific strategies are needed when children's misbehavior ties up all parental energies. These strategies incorporate understanding of the child's history of maltreatment, the survival function of his symptoms, his distorted perceptions of relationships, and his maturational age, among other variables (see previous chapter). Given the resistance to change and the need for control that many troubled children demonstrate, many of the following strategies employ elements of playfulness, surprise, gentle shaping, paradox and/or reverse psychology. Rather than utilizing a "bigger hammer" to drive home a point with the child, these approaches attempt to tap certain key issues deftly.

The list of sixteen sample strategies follows:

1. Adopting Your Hormonal Teenage Son's Girlfriend
2. Gentle Shaping
3. Disarming with Humor
4. Putting Words in Their Mouths
5. Pledge of Allegiance
6. Coming Half the Distance
7. Description-Interpretation-Confrontation-Explanation
8. Daily Press Conference
9. Lullaby for the Lonely Heart
10. Pavlov's Blankey
11. Ask Me No Questions
12. Make a Wish
13. My Backpack on My Back

14. Fun-filled Eating
15. Midnight Snack at 3 A.M.
16. My Voice Journeys with You

(These strategies are offered as illustrations of how unorthodox family strategies can make inroads with the troubled child. The strategies are not meant to be a cookbook of solutions, but rather as illustrations of formulating problems and addressing difficulties. Other sample strategies have been described elsewhere for other behavioral issues [Delaney, 1996; Kunstal and Delaney, 1993]. It is strongly recommended that any and all unorthodox strategies be pro-active, legal, child-sensitive, and developed jointly by the therapeutic team.)

1. Adopting Your Hormonal Teenage Son's Girlfriend

A worried, single adoptive mother came to her parent support group with a most interesting problem. Her fourteen-year-old, adopted son disappeared each night to run to his girlfriend's house for sex. This nightly erotic pilgrimage had her worried. The girlfriend, an unsupervised thirteen-year-old, lived with a negligent mother who looked the other way, in effect, when the boy and girl disappeared into the bedroom.

The adoptive mother had tried a number of interventions to no avail. She had, for instance, attempted to physically stand in the way of her son when he left at night. However, that proved to be somewhat hazardous, as he was much taller and stronger than she. The mother had also tried to reason with the boy, appealing to morals, religious values, health issues, and the very real danger of being out after dark on the mean streets of a big city. (This last issue was extremely important. Her son had been chased on foot by several gang members, when he crossed their turf without permission. In another instance, he had nearly been caught in the cross-fire of rival gangs disputing drug trade in the vicinity.)

Worried primarily about her son's health and safety, the adoptive mother came up with the notion that she would have to drive him to the girlfriend's house herself, wait for him in the car, and then chauffeur him back home after the nightly tryst. Out of ideas, she remarked, "What else can I do, short of permitting him to risk life and limb?"

The adoptive parent support group came up with other options and questions to consider:

1. Could she enlist the support of the girlfriend's mother? The adoptive mother replied that this woman had refused to discuss the concerns and seemed content that she knew where her daughter was every night (e.g. in the bedroom!).

2. Could she report the runaway behavior to the sheriff or police? The adoptive mother stated that she had called officers out to talk to her

son. However, law enforcement appeared disinterested in the matter, since the boy was not a true runaway.

3. Could she help find a girlfriend for the boy, who lived closer to the home? The adoptive mother found this suggestion ironic. In effect, would she help her son find a more conveniently located sexual partner?

4. Had she considered using the natural consequences method? That is, why not let the boy continue to risk his safety, but let him bear the consequences, even if that meant that he got injured. Some in the group found this to be too cavalier, akin to leaving the matter to fate.

When it appeared that the support group had run out of ideas, three more emerged.

5. Since the girlfriend has no viable, guiding mother figure, the adoptive mother could reach out to this child. More specifically, she could invite her over to the house to dine with her son and herself. In the process, the adoptive mother could have the girl help her prepare dinner, talk with her, and develop a surrogate mother-daughter relationship. As a result, she would have the opportunity to supervise her son and newly "adopted" daughter.

6. Report the girlfriend's mother to the authorities for neglect.

7. Involve the adopted son in more pro-social, age-appropriate activities to redirect his sexual energies. Consider a Big Brother relationship to steer him into fulfilling, non-sexual activity.

At the next monthly support group meeting, the adoptive mother reported that she had successfully engaged the girlfriend. A close, surrogate mother-daughter relationship had begun to develop. The mother stated, "At first, I was doing this for my son. But soon I found out how enjoyable Melissa was. She's a sweet girl really, lonely for a mother. Sometimes she would show up when my son wasn't even around, just to talk. One night, when my son winked at her to signal it was time to slink off and be sexual with him, Melissa stood up to him, 'Can't you see I'm talking with Mom?'"

In adopting her hormonal, teenaged son's girlfriend, the adoptive mother had brought more responsibility her way. It did permit a closer form of supervising his adolescent behavior. However, as might be expected, her son jilted Melissa in favor of another sexually active girl. The adoptive mother stated, "I guess I'll be starting up a sorority in my home." Fortunately, she never had to go that far, since involvement with a Big Brother helped her son sublimate his sex drive appropriately.

Sometimes treating problem behaviors entails use of
the gentle cycle.

2. Gentle Shaping

In many problems, we find the seeds of solution. Rather than attempting a whole-sale expunging of a problem behavior, we may find more success in gently shaping troublesome activity into more appropriate actions, as in the following case:

A group home for developmentally disabled youth had a serious public relations problem. They had not been well-received by the upscale neighborhood when they first bought the large home, converted it, and moved in twelve disturbed, lower functioning teenaged boys. Local homeowners were predictably concerned about property values going down and crime rates going up. After two years without any major problems, however, the group home was seen as a curiosity, not a threat, and neighborhood paranoia had subsided. Then an unforeseen problem emerged. The main sewer line down the street from the group home had plugged and backed up, regurgitating sewage back into the homes from which it came. The neighbors were not amused when informed by the sanitation department that a large clot of soggy clothing and towels with "Acme Group Home" stamped on them had been unearthed in the stopped up sewer pipes.

After some initial detective work, the group home staff found the culprit. A fourteen-year-old boy with autistic-like features had an interesting compulsion. He loved to watch towels swirl round and round in the toilet bowl. Routinely, and perhaps even daily, he visited the bathroom with towels and articles of clothing hidden under his shirt. Then, he proceeded to throw the articles in the bowl and flush them away one at a time. He delighted in witnessing articles swirling around the toilet before they disappeared.

The staff resisted the expected tendency to punish or expunge this problem. They did not, for example, lock "Mr. Swirly" out of the bathrooms, place a sentinel at each washroom door, or even assign an escort to tail him throughout the day. Instead, they prescribed periods of swirling during the day, with some important modifications. Mr. Swirly was allowed to swirl clothing and wash-rags, etc. in the bathroom sink. Three times per day, for one-half hour each, a staff member monitored the swirling in the sink, allowing Mr. Swirly to enjoy the entire process of stirring the articles in a full sink with a stick. After using the sink for one week, the location of swirling was changed to a large bucket placed on the floor of the bathroom. Once again for seven days, three times per day, thirty minutes each, Mr. Swirly was directed to stir and swirl clothing, etc. in the bucket. Next, in the third week, the swirling was moved down to the main hallway. Last, Mr. Swirly was taken to the laundry room off the main hallway, where he was taught to wash and dry clothing. He found himself in "swirling heaven" with this task. Especially with the ultimate swirling experience of the clothing spinning in the washing machines and dryers.

Sometimes treating problem behaviors entails using the gentle cycle. Elimination of problems does not necessarily require punishment or confrontation. Gentle shaping of the problem behavior, once we understand the need behind the problem, may channel the individual in a mutually acceptable activity.

In many situations it is helpful to "meet the child where he is at." If we restrain the urge to expect immediate change, if we can reduce the sense of impatience to normalize children, we often find a more gradual pace for change which the child will not sandbag, or for that matter, flush down the toilet.

Humor can defuse volatile situations.

3. Disarming with Humor

Foster and adoptive parents claim that a good sense of humor is essential to surviving and thriving with troubled children. A sense of humor can really come in handy, especially if you are the parent of a troubled child. Now, this sense of humor does not mean you are Seinfeld, Robin Williams, or a 1990's version of Groucho Marx. You do not have to be the life of every party, nor must you have a quick, witty comment for every parent-child interaction.

What is needed is not only a sense of humor, but a sense of irony, a sense of amusement, and the ability to detect the humor in a wide range of situations. The child cannot see the humorous side of these situations because of his rigidity, fearfulness, or tunnel vision. At those times, humor can defuse volatile situations; it can loosen the rigid defenses of a child who is on edge around adults. And, it may infuse the ridiculous into encounters which otherwise might remain fearsome or contentious to the child, as in the following case:

A foster mother called me from a southern state to share her spontaneous approach to a tense situation with her ten-year-old foster daughter. The girl had been riding in the driveway, when she took a spill. For some reason, this became the impetus for her to stomp off and run away from the house, which luckily was ten miles outside of the nearest small town. The foster mother watched the girl march further and further away from the home, wondering how she might intervene without getting into a chase with the child. Then, she spotted the girl's small bike. The lightbulb went on. Positioning her rather large form onto this petite bike, she pedaled after the child and caught up with her, but did not attempt to stop her. Without saying a word, the foster mother, dwarfing the bike, made lazy circles around the child who walked only a bit further. The child then gave up, turned around and marched back home, with the foster mother silently pedaling along side.

Using levity during the above crisis allowed the foster mother to sidestep being drawn into the child's misbehavior. Indeed, the playfulness indicated a certain clinical distance, which signaled that the foster mother was not personally offended or impacted negatively by the child. The sight of the foster mother on the bike took the edge off the seriousness and turned the child around, figuratively and literally.

The notion of putting words in children's mouths is loathsome to most mental health and helping professionals.

4. Putting Words in Their Mouths

Traditional, non-directive therapy approaches with children have serious limitations when employed with troubled foster and adopted children. This is especially true when the clock is ticking and when issues arising in the home threaten placement stability and longevity.

In some instances we do not have the luxury of time to allow children's central issues to emerge at their own pace. Indeed, in some instances, adhering to complete non-direction we might never touch issues which the child studiously avoids. In these cases, we simply must more directly educate and actively bring the non-insightful, emotionally-illiterate child closer to his inner workings. More specifically, we may need to "put words in the child's mouth." By this approach, we identify the feelings the child would be expected to experience in a specific situation. In the chronic absence of verbal expression of feelings by the troubled child, we vocalize the issues/feelings for him or her.

Admittedly, the notion of putting words in children's mouths is loathesome to most mental health and helping professionals. In our training, in our beliefs, we honor the child's need to express himself without pressure. In the therapeutic climate of unconditional acceptance and patience, the child is expected to emerge in all his truthful individuality. However, work with troubled foster and adopted children usually demands a more active therapist role. More attempts are necessary to escort the child into areas which he otherwise would walk away from, as in the following illustration:

According to his adoptive mother, eleven-year-old Timothy was the "Sultan of Shrugs," by which she meant that he met every question about himself, his feelings or opinions, with a smirk, a shrug, and an "I don't know." Timothy had been quite upset about the fact that another foster child in the home had returned to his biological parents, while he (Timothy) remained in care indefinitely. He was very upset with his birth father who attested that he wanted to win back custody, but ironically failed to visit consistently or to fulfill his court appointed treatment plan. (The birth mother had abandoned Timothy years before, and her whereabouts were unknown.) Timothy denied anger at his father, but acted out secret anger through urinating on the floor of his bedroom and by fire-

setting in the neighborhood. This acting out had increased dramatically when his birth father's visits began to taper off.

After a discussion between the caseworker, foster parents, and therapist, the therapist began to confront the painful issues which the boy had shunned: his father's increasingly spotty visitation and markedly lackluster commitment to his son.

The therapist remarked, in the absence of verbalized feelings from Timothy, "Tim, you seem to be saying by your behavior that you are angry that your father has almost totally stopped visiting you." Tim responded by, of course, shrugging and turning away from the therapist's gaze. Undeterred, the therapist proceeded, "It doesn't seem fair that, as hard as you have tried in the foster home to work on your problems, your father hasn't worked on his treatment plan." Tim scowled, but remained speechless. The therapist forged ahead gently but firmly, "If I were you, I might worry that if I told my father how angry I was at him about his performance, he might never visit me again...Yes, if I were you, Tim, I'd be wondering whether he wanted me back at all." Finally, turning to face the therapist directly, Tim glared angrily and spoke up, "You don't know what you are talking about! My dad doesn't visit because he has car problems!" The therapist gently, but persistently, said, "Tim, I know you love your father, but sometimes we are furious with the ones we love the most. Especially, when they let us down or disappoint us, like your dad has disappointed you."

In the above, the therapist has introduced feelings, ideas, and thoughts which Tim has either felt and not expressed or which he poorly understands. Truly, the therapist has put words in Tim's mouth, which the boy has summarily rejected. Even though Tim has rejected the therapist's version of his feelings, the fact that Tim has even vocalized a defense of his father may be superior to his earlier smirking, shrugging, and silence.

The approach illustrated above may be valuable with the following children:

> 1. The child who chronically cannot label feelings and has no emotional insight;

> 2. The child who characteristically avoids expressing feelings and even refuses to articulate them; and

3. The child who typically speaks through behavior rather than words.

The objectives of this approach include the following:

1. To actively increase a child's emotional vocabulary;

2. To vocalize for the child some of his/her unspoken feelings; and

3. To push buttons which the child refuses to push in himself.

(Note: Therapists, caseworkers, or foster/adoptive parents should use this approach advisedly, and in concert with the treatment team efforts. When the child is involved in court proceedings related to abuse, special caution should be taken not to force admissions on the child or to foster the development of false memories.)

The sharing of the nightly pledge of allegiance allowed an opening in the child's heart for the adoptive mother.

5. Pledge of Allegiance

A particularly touchy issue is that of the remaining loyalty to, as well as the persistent idealization of, birth parents by the foster or adopted child. Foster and adoptive parents almost universally report difficulties in helping the child to establish a close, meaningful relationship with them, due, in great part, to the feelings of loyalty to the birth mother and/or father. The allegiance to the birth parents can effectively stymie the formation of helpful, curative ties to the foster or adoptive parents. This can happen even when the birth parents have abandoned the child or are out of the picture completely. Foster and adoptive children continue to cherish the memories and at times canonize into sainthood the hallowed reminiscences of the birth parents. This can be true even when abuse, neglect and sexual exploitation ran rampant in the relationship. Indeed, foster or adoptive children who were most abused or neglected often times hold on more stubbornly (cf. "The Least Favored Child" in chapter 2) to unrealistic dreams of reunification and to over-idealized recollections of the birth parent, as seen in the following:

Reggie, a ten-year-old foster/adoptive boy, had been placed with his two older brothers in a home with two inexperienced adoptive parents. After a year in the family, a termination of birth parents' rights had been completed and the appeal ended. The boys were free for adoption. While the older boys seemed eager to move towards a finalization, Reggie showed resistance to the idea. Ironically, Reggie had been the least favored of the boys in his family of origin. Neglected from birth, Reggie exhibited failure to thrive. When placed in foster care for the first time he had lost nearly all his teeth due to malnutrition, and his buttocks were covered with bruises of various ages.

In the present foster/adoptive home, Reggie had balked at belonging. Although he interacted passably well with the adoptive father, he had an extremely contentious relationship to the adoptive mother. Each time she attempted to engage him in any positive way, Reggie would torpedo her efforts. In psychotherapy, Reggie's play showed themes of the continuing desire to reunite with his birth mother, whom he sanctified. She was, in his view, the perfect mother. During therapy, Reggie also complained bitterly about his adoptive mother, whom he viewed as mean, cruel, and unfair. The split of "good mother-bad mother" was stark. In effect, Reggie denied, repressed, and split-off *his anger at the birth mother for her chronic maltreatment of him. At the same time, Reggie displaced those angry feelings onto the safe target of the adoptive mother. While protecting his age-old hope that he might some day have a good relationship with his birth mother, this displacement served to keep the adoptive mother at bay. Reggie did not have to develop a real relationship that felt threatening and foreign to him.*

With all this going on, the adoptive mother felt unable to reach Reggie in any satisfying, positive way. She was rebuffed even when she attempted out-of-the-ordinary ways of reaching Reggie. For instance, when she spent extra time reading and talking with Reggie at bedtime, he would sometimes hide under the covers or would pretend not to listen. When the adoptive mother reached out to hold, rock or hug Reggie at bedtime, he immediately drew back and brought up recollections about his birth mother.

Naturally, the adoptive mother felt totally discouraged by Reggie's stiff-armed approach. She found the nightly rejection at bedtime especially devastating.

The advice from her adoptive-parent support group was to acknowledge rather than thwart the recollection process. She was encouraged to use an intervention which would put the adoptive mother in the role of supporting the positive feelings the child held toward his birth mother. This would increase the child's ability to develop an awareness of the negatives felt toward his birth mother. The ultimate goal would be to permit the child to embrace reality and to grow more positively attached to the adoptive mother.

After further discussion, the "Pledge of Allegiance to the Birth Mother" strategy was developed. In it the adoptive mother would not wait for the child to stiff-arm her and voice his loyalty to the birth mother. Instead, she took the initiative and became the most loyal follower of the birth mother. "Reggie, it's bedtime. I know you start to recall your Mom at this time when I come in. From what you have told me about her, she must have been a wonderful mother. I know she missed some visits with you near the end, but I'm sure she loves you just the same." Without totally excusing the birth mother's lapses, deficiencies, and ultimate abandonment, the adoptive mother joined the child in his routine idealization (and missing) of his birth mother. Without exonerating past maltreatment, the adoptive mother voiced the child's own rationalizations of his birth mother's misbehavior, leaving him with less need to defend her. She verbalized for him his continuing loyalty and dreams of reuniting with her, relieving him of the need to emphasize that on-going alliance.

By the use of this paradoxical approach, the adoptive mother places herself in the child's camp. Ironically, she also allows him to reduce his automatic defensiveness and distortion of reality. Interestingly, in this specific case when the adoptive mother joined her son in this fashion, it made it easier for him to grieve, crying for his birth mother. In very touching ways, he then allowed the adoptive mother to embrace, comfort and console him in those moments. The sharing of the nightly pledge of allegiance allowed an opening in the child's heart for the adoptive mother.

6. Coming Half the Distance: When to Require Effort from Your Adopted Child

Some adopting families are hamstrung by their very commitment to adopt. That is, children with attachment problems may manipulate other's commitment toward them. They may feel free of any responsibility to make a reciprocal commitment to the family or to some of its members.

In one Canadian case, a thirteen-year-old boy, Billy, became available for adoption to Mr. and Mrs. Stemple, his foster/adoptive parents of two years. While the foster parents were dedicated to the plan to adopt, the foster mother reported distress in her relationship to her prospective adoptive son. This boy gave her no respect, routinely ignoring her and actively resisting her efforts to parent, discipline or guide him. To Billy, women and mothers were unimportant, unworthy, second class life forms. He had been raised in a family of origin where his birth mother was a battered, masochistic, impotent woman who commanded zero respect from her husband and/or children. Billy's view of mothers/women had remained unaltered throughout his foster care years. His disrespect and defiance toward adult females at home (and school) mushroomed as he grew physically larger. Additionally, his anger toward the female sex reared its ugly head routinely. Billy yelled at his foster mother to "shut up" or immaturely covered his ears when she talked to him. The therapist suggested that the foster mother ignore Billy at these times, in the hope that he would eventually reach out to her to communicate. However, this meeting "fire with fire" approach had failed to produce change. Billy persistently blocked her out. Perhaps, it gave Billy exactly what he wanted or expected from a mother, e.g. nothing.

Not all of the defiant/hostile behavior from Billy was as benign as ignoring and generic disrespect. Once, when Mrs. Stemple disconnected the television set, which Billy had been watching into the wee hours of the night against her wishes, Billy smashed her CD player in "tit for tat" fashion. This escalated acting out frightened Mrs. Stemple, rendering her more reluctant than ever to adopt a strong parental position. In a nutshell, she felt intimidated.

In contrast to his wife's "Rodney Dangerfield role," Mr. Stemple experienced a wholly different relationship to Billy. His foster son deferred to him, followed his directions, and only presented nominal, normal teenaged rebellion.

In this case, it was clear that Billy needed to hear from both foster parents that the adoption process would be indefinitely placed on hold until he could work toward a resolution of his feelings toward his foster mother. Billy would have to connect with and get along with his foster mother, e.g. to come half the distance in the relationship. The foster parents were encouraged to emphasize the fact that the adoption would only occur when and if Billy accepted both parents. Any fantasy Billy held about adoption by Mr. Stemple alone would be confronted. Mr. Stemple would emphatically state to Billy that he could only be adopted by both parents. In this process of confrontation, Billy would also be confronted about his unequal treatment of his foster mother and of women in general.

Lastly, if Billy could not accept the arrangement of adoption by two parents, he may need a temporary respite placement elsewhere to contemplate whether he might work toward accepting a father, and a mother.

7. Description, Interpretation, Confrontation, and Explanation

At times we needlessly keep children in the dark about what we know about them. For example, the recurrent themes, the self-defeating patterns and the irresponsible habits they show so evidently. Uninformed, in the dark, and ignorant about himself, the child may act in ways which are self-defeating. This is particularly true when the child defeats those who love him; then everyone loses.

Clarisse, an eleven-year-old foster child, was a professional victim. A budding masochist, she had become quite adept at setting others up to mistreat and reject her. This confirmed her worst preconceptions about others and herself. History revealed that Clarisse had been a miracle baby, a low birth weight infant who nearly died because of medical problems early-on. She survived respiratory and digestive problems, and she thrived physically through her toddler-hood and preschool years. However, behavior problems erupted with a vengeance at the age of three-and- a-half. At that time her twin baby brothers were born with their own health problems. This took attention away from her and shifted parental overprotection away from her and toward the twins.

Clarisse became the consummate negative attention-seeker. She was insanely jealous of her twin brothers, going so far as to carry one of them out to the busy thoroughfare which passed by their home. The biological parents, witnessing this "homicidal" act, sent Clarisse to live with her grandmother. However, behavior problems escalated further in that home. Clarisse was next placed in a series of foster families, none of which could reach the child. Eventually, birth parents relinquished rights to Clarisse and she was placed in a therapeutic foster/adoptive home at the age of ten.

One year later, now eleven, Clarisses' adoption was not yet finalized because of continuing behavioral problems. In this placement, Clarisse would defecate while in "time out," and she rubbed phlegm and nasal secretions on the walls and bed sheets. At school, Clarisse routinely would set others up to hit her. She called her teacher, a f—ing bitch. Oddly, Clarisse was the only child who had a lock on her locker, but the lock was broken. It was an odd attention seeking behavior and an open invitation to others to inspect and open her locker. The double message of the broken lock seemed to be: "Stay out of my locker....violate my locker." The broken lock invited the curious, potential thief. This puzzling behavior was a peculiar form of acting out. It was a request to be mistreated by those who might violate her locker, and simultaneously it was an attempt to entrap. Specifically, Clarisse baited the other children with her locker. If they took the bait and opened her locker, she immediately reported them to the principal.

What can be done to help Clarisse surrender this ill-advised, masochistic behavior? Therapist, caseworker, teacher, and foster/adoptive parents may need to work in concert to describe, interpret, confront, and explain to Clarisse what her queer locker-behavior (and other behavior) communicates to others. The adults, wise to Clarisse's modus operandi can verbalize and perhaps even write out for Clarisse in explicit, narrative form how she sets herself up for negative encounters with other children. In this way, we may help this girl understand and control her own misbehavior. We might describe her life's history and explain the self-defeating patterns she has developed. We might weave in the following interpretations: You have always needed much attention and you deserved it. When you have not been able to get it, you have found other ways to grab it, even if it was negative attention. You have resented other children, since they remind you of the painful loss of your parents' attention when the twins came along. Getting other children in troubled has brought some sense of satisfaction, but has also set you up for rejection by them.

The use of description, interpretation, confrontation, and explanation (not unlike approaches espoused by narrative therapists) can be utilized when the child is not putting two and two together about how he acts, why he misbehaves, and the reasons behind his self-defeating activities. At times, it is highly valuable for the therapist, caseworker, and/or parents to "do the math," to add things up for the child.

8. Daily Press Conference

S ome troubled children have an insatiable need to remain fully informed, on top of things, and privy to all that happens in their world. Well beyond curiosity, there is an obsessive, hyper-vigilant, snoopy quality to their interest, as seen in the following case:

Barbara was a ten-year-old adopted girl who had to know everything. Anxious about her world, she was perpetually in a "need to know" posture with everyone and every situation. Controlling with her sisters, she could provoke them to get into fights with each other. She was unable to interact competently with peers, given her inability to keep a friend because of her tendency to dominate in all relationships. In the family she competed with an older brother over the parent role in the house. The adoptive parents found themselves unable to have a simple conversation with each other without Barbara eavesdropping. She was relentless in her need to pry and to listen in on their communications with each other. In her early life before foster and adoptive care, she had been surrounded by danger. Survival was a central issue in her life. Additionally, Barbara had been the guardian of family secrets - secrets about abuse and neglect.

Barbara's anxiety, eavesdropping and controlling behavior had dramatically increased with the development of certain factors. The adoptive mother was preoccupied and concerned about her older son. This son lived out of the city and was going through a rough time in his life. He had made a suicide gesture and was isolating himself. Additionally, the adoptive mother had lost her father after a long terminal illness and was depressed about this. The adoptive mother's withdrawal and depression alarmed Barbara, who had often assumed a role-inverted relationship to her birth mother who was quite unstable and needy.

The caseworker advised the adoptive parents to dramatically increase the sharing of information with Barbara. It was recommended that, in effect, the adoptive parents provide daily "press conferences" for Barbara, in which they would keep her updated on the schedule, upcoming events, and especially on the emotional climate of key individuals in the house. The purpose of the conferences for Barbara was to clarify the facts and let her know what to expect. She would receive reassurance that the adoptive mother's depression was not caused by Barbara and that it was not Barbara's fault that the older brother was struggling. The objectives of the daily press conferences were:

1. To explain to Barbara: "It's not you."

2. To provide the essentials about what is happening but not too much detail about the suicide attempt.

3. To reassure her: "Mother is not angry at you...it is not your fault or responsibility. You don't have to fix things."

4. To confirm: "We are not going to hurt you or leave you."

5. To permit the adoptive mother to reveal some of her own feelings and communicate to Barbara: "You don't need to take care of me. But I sure could use a hug right now. I just wanted to share with you that I'm okay."

Daily press conferences would allow this child to get the information she previously had to sneak to get. These conferences would share basic information, and more importantly give reassurance to a girl who was not used to sharing feelings and having open dialogue about family crises.

Overall, the practice of offering regular, open disclosure within the family provides the troubled foster or adopted child with general family information, updated household status reports, and unfolding future plans. The result will be an overall sense of reduced anxiety about what is in store for him/her.

9. Lullaby for the Lonely Heart

Self-parenting is the quintessential symptom of children who have been neglected or have been raised without parenting in early life. Exposure to abandonment, under-stimulation, and inadequate, low quality parenting can predispose children to self-parenting. If the child has been neglected by a substance-abusing parent, or if the infant has been raised in a substandard orphanage, the results may be the same. The child learns to parent his/herself.

The following case illustrates that some self-stimulation and self-soothing are examples of parenting one's self:

A two-year-old boy, a foster child who was sorely neglected in the first eighteen months of his life, seemed fixated on "self-soothing" behavior. He would rock and drone to himself at various times during the day. Though he had been living in a nurturing foster home for six months, the droning and rocking continued. The foster mother questioned whether she should allow this behavior or interrupt it.

In talking with the foster mother, she reported that when she sang to her foster son, he almost instantly fell into a peaceful sleep, especially if she rocked him in her arms. This bit of information, along with the history of neglect and lack of external stimulation from past parent figures presented the information needed to develop an intervention. Specifically, it was suggested that the foster mother continue her singing and rocking as before, and that she increase this form of mothering. When her foster son would begin to rock and drone, she should see it as her cue to offer mothering. Her goal was to replace self-soothing with good mothering.

In this situation, a foster or adoptive parent needs to read the behavior and recognize it as an opportunity. The self-stimulation should be viewed as a green light, an indicator that the child is parenting himself.

Unfortunately, when the child self-parents, the foster or adoptive parent is out of the loop. At these times, the parent needs to insert his/herself into this solitary pursuit. Once successfully engaged with the child, it is possible to teach the child that the parent can offer comfort, soothing and security - that the child can turn to others for solace. Solace, rather than solitary, is what we are after. Additionally, we are wanting the child to be able to identify when he needs others, as well as when and how to ask for what he needs.

10. Pavlov's Blankey

Recent press coverage has informed us that infants adopted from orphanages in third world nations have often experienced a great deal of trauma and injury. Adopting post-institution or street children is a praiseworthy and humanitarian effort. However, many families who have adopted infants out of orphanage care, (e.g. infants who were abandoned, babies who were neglected and malnourished) have found that those infants and young children carry internal scars - intellectual, psychological - which heal slowly if at all.

One couple who adopted Baby Ronnie at about two years of age from China found him to be passive and limp, though in general his health seemed good. He had scars on both wrists and both ankles - rope burns left from restraints used in the orphanage. When the little boy first arrived at his home in the United States, he could not sleep without a tattered, grimy towel in his hand, the only memento from the institution. This was his transitional object, his security blanket. To sleep, he had to hold this in one hand, suck on it with his mouth while lightly caressing it with the other hand. Clutching his soiled cloth, he would drift comfortably off to sleep. He needed no lullaby, no rocking, no bedtime hug and kiss. Indeed, in his nightly autistic state, he seemingly needed no mother or father.

The adoptive couple, following the advice of the adoption agency, attempted to insert themselves into this child's "autistic" world. Throughout the day they held him almost constantly, attempting to make up for lost time. He was rarely left alone and was carried on the mother or father's hip from dawn to dusk. At bedtime, they instituted a comforting ritual with cuddling, soothing, singing, and rocking him to sleep. As a result of this labor of love, the child was clearly forming a bond - so far, so good.

As the child approached three-years-of-age the couple felt that a mutual attachment was developing between them and the child. However, the adoptive parents were concerned that their son was, in their words, "too attached." They reported that he still insisted on bottle-feeding, although he also accepted some baby foods and solids. Moreover, they grew increasingly alarmed by his sleep problem. He had become conditioned to a nightly bedtime ritual which included rocking him to sleep and putting him in their bed. If they tried to put him in his crib to sleep alone, he screamed and carried *on until they picked him back up and/or placed him in bed with them. Even after confined in his room, alone and crying, for three hours the child had not relented. The couple caved in, and brought Ronnie back into the marital bedroom. The pediatrician recommended medication for the child, knocking him out at bedtime, but short of that the family had run out of ideas.*

The questions to ask at this moment are: Do the parents have legitimate concerns about the sleep problem? Have they, as they put it, "created a monster" vis a vis bedtime? Specifically, will they do irreparable harm to their son by letting him sleep with them?

Robert Wright (author, The Moral Animal: Evolutionary Psychology and Everyday Life) attacks what he dubs, "the boot camp for babies" notion of insisting that babies and young children, must, at all costs learn to sleep independently. Sleeping with children has, in the minds of some experts seemed perverse, strictly taboo, akin to emotional incest, or at least interfering with the child's attainment of nocturnal self-reliance. This may be bunk in the view of Robert Wright. Programs which rely on letting baby cry itself to sleep may be traumatic to the normal baby. Why must we be so harsh in our process of teaching the baby/child to sleep alone, when there are gentler approaches? Proponents of the "family bed" have reportedly found great success in including their children in the marital bed. Even parents who do not espouse the "family bed" idea, inevitably have slept with their sick, frightened, nightmaring children, and they know instinctively how comforting it is for their offspring to be with mom and/or dad in the night.

Far from "creating a monster" (in the case of Ronnie), the adoptive parents had done a masterful job of forming attachments between themselves and their child. Admittedly, the nature of the attachment is insecure, but preferable to the parentless position the child entered the home with. No longer is the child content with self-imposed solitary confinement. Now he needs and demands parent involvement!

Still, the adoptive parents' question about how to proceed with the bedtime issue is valid. Should they be content with bedtime as usual or should they press for changes in the child? Yes, they might need to press for changes if sleeping with the child affects them negatively (for example, if they cannot sleep or if they have not been able to maintain a conjugal relationship). However, the answer is "no" if we are strictly focused on the child's development and if we're trying to properly encourage change to happen naturally, without acute resistance from Ronnie.

In the case of our little adoptee, it might be wise for the couple to allow him to sleep with them in their bed for several months or more. What can it hurt? During that period these parents might try some classical conditioning. Bring back a security blanket of some sort. The child had created his own (the frayed towel) in the orphanage, which had been taken away by the parents. In its place now, the parents could bundle the child up in a soft blanket, and rock the child in their arms swaddled in this comfortable cloth. An experienced foster/ adoptive mother suggested to me once, that mothers should continuously wear a perfume and father, a cologne, around the insecure child and should lightly scent the child's blankey or teddy bear with the same fragrance. The sense of smell and the olfactory triggered memories have a powerful impact on all humans. The gradual conditioning of the blankey to the familiar scent of the mother and father produces a soothing "Pavlov's Blankey." The blankey becomes comforting by association and may help the child in learning to sleeping alone.

In any case, the adoptive parents in this scenario need reassurance that they have done well with their new son. They also need specific advice on how to proceed less apprehensively in the gradual unfolding of Ronnie's capacity to sleep alone.

Note: Foster parents should note that state regulations often prohibit children from sleeping with parents. Both foster and adoptive parents should use caution when developing bedtime strategies with children who have been sexual abuse victims.

11. Ask Me No Questions, I'll Tell Ye No Lies

Children who lie undermine the trust that a family requires. Trust and truth are the bedrock of close relationships. However, some children torpedo relationships by lying frequently or almost constantly. The act of deceit in these children seems effortless and almost reflexive. Ironically, telling the truth appears to demand more energy.

When children have become habitual liars, many parents and professionals are uncertain about how to deal with the problem, as seen in the following case:

When a full bag of candy disappeared from the kitchen cupboard, Mr. and Mrs. Brown immediately knew that the culprit was Jimmy. The only child in the home, Jimmy, who was adopted at age 5 and was now 7, was an inveterate thief. His dedication to thievery was matched by his compulsion to deny the truth and to reject taking responsibility.

On the advice of their therapist, the Browns had recently ceased their typical approach of confronting Jimmy about stealing. Whenever they asked him why or if he had stolen, they received only shrugs, alibis or bold face prevarication. In truth, the Browns almost never exacted a confession or admission. Rather than achieving more honesty in the relationship with Jimmy, they felt he was actually, with practice, growing more skilled at lying straight-faced.

The new approach meticulously avoided any discussion of the details of the case. The parents were to merely inform Jimmy about what they were certain he had stolen and to mete out consequences for the act. They allowed no debate, explanation, or lying.

Using the new, "don't ask" approach, the Browns found that Billy became quite emotional. At times he spoke honestly about his chronic sense of never getting enough, about life's unfairness, and about what he perceived as parental stinginess. This form of emotional honesty was viewed as bona fide progress.

In intervening on behalf of children like Jimmy, who lie and deny constantly, consider the following:

1. Parents may have to accept less than perfectly truthful behavior, in the hope that over time the child will become more truthful. It may be unrealistic to expect impeccable honesty in the short run.

2. It may be mandatory to avoid cross examination and debate with children who automatically lie to save their skins. Sometimes when we question, examine, and grill the child, he will either shut down or improve his skills of denial, argument, and prevarication.

3. In approaching the child who habitually lies, parents should eliminate questions and in their place, make declarative statements, presenting the child with their understanding of the facts. Following that, they should not allow the child to provide explanations, especially if he is an accomplished liar. (Ironically, if we squelch the opportunity that the child has to bend the truth, he might like Jimmy, become exasperated and tell us how he really feels, e.g. "You never believe me...you believe the other kids and always take their side...you love them better than me!")

4. Foster or adoptive parents may need to encourage more overall, outward, verbal expression from the child. They should seek more general candor about anger, thought and opinions. There is a strong correlation between lying about the facts and dishonesty about feelings. The lack of "truth-telling" is often associated with an absence of candor about emotions. With that in mind, one avenue to general truthfulness is through more honest expression of emotion, both positive and negative.

12. Make a Wish

Some foster and adoptive children feel so disappointed and pessimistic about life that they refuse to have wants, to dream dreams, or to expect anything. Their motto is: If you don't expect much, you won't be disappointed.

With one teenaged boy, his life appeared sapped of energy. He looked depressed but denied feeling that way. At the same time, he had no future orientation. Life droned on and he with it, but without joy, without anything to look forward to. With his history of dashed hopes and broken promises, was he beyond wishing, hoping and dreaming?

Some children are so tied up with issues from the past and with confusion in the present, that they lack the energy to deal with a future. Indeed, the future is burdensome and frightening. Instead of providing something to strive for, to long for, to get excited about, and to draw meaning from, the future frightens, overwhelms, and intimidates.

Barbara was a sixteen-year-old foster child without a wishbone - a youngster with no secret garden. Although not clinically depressed, Barbara lacked enthusiasm, vision or even chutzpah. According to her foster parents, she was "a robot with lungs, lips and a birth certificate." She lived in "the now" mechanically. Barbara was not meditative nor particularly calm in her "now" world. She wasn't truly enjoying each moment in the present. Sadly, her past had soured her, and in effect had obliterated her sense of future. Her foster mother, an enthusiastic, bustling woman with energy to spare, was initially puzzled and incredulous about Barbara's lack of future. This energetic woman would not let it drop. She coached Barbara incessantly on how to hope and daydreamed out loud with her: "Barbara, let's plan what we'll do this evening...this weekend..this summer...Where should we go on our summer car trip? ...Barbara, what are you going to be when you grow up?"

We need to help kids realize that, in the words of Yogi Berra, "The future ain't what it used to be." Their tomorrows don't need to be rehashed versions of their yesterdays. We should encourage them to plan, to expect, to hope for, and to dream. More basically, we need to teach them how to think ahead, not just so they are more plan-full and less impulsive and rash, but so they can derive pleasure from the future.

The backpack was described as a way to remind Jamie that her needs were important and would be met.

13. My Backpack on My Back

Food issues are frequently paramount in the lives of many foster and adopted children. Whether these children have been starved physically or underfed emotionally, the gnawing sense of emptiness consumes them.

To address their historic emptiness, these youngsters often turn to food to fill the void. Pilfering food, hoarding it in secret caches, and gorging to the point of gluttony are common. Food itself becomes an obsession. Where will my next meal come from? Does anyone feed me properly? Do people understand what I need physically, emotionally? Does anyone really care about me? These are all questions which the love-starved, food obsessed child raises continuously.

Janie had lived with the Noble foster family for eight months. She was a seven-year-old, formerly neglected girl, raised by a clinically depressed and often substance-abusing mother. Janie had been left to raise herself and to take care of her own needs. She did not look to her birth mother as the source of sustenance, nor did she count on her to provide three square meals a day.

Eight months into the foster placement, Janie, even though she was fed very adequately, persisted in stealing and hoarding food on a daily basis. Mr. and Mrs. Noble discovered decomposing food under the bed, dozens of candy wrappers stuffed down the heat vents, and many objects missing from their pantry.

Quizzing Janie about the evidence found in her room and asking her about what she'd like to eat during mealtimes produced few positive results. The constant obsession with food and the squirreling away of foods continued unabated. Finally, Janie's psychotherapist suggested that the family tangibly provide Janie with the feeling of fullness and the sense of security that she heretofore lacked. A strategy was employed which entailed using a backpack filled by Janie with food stuffs which would satisfy her needs. She selected some sweets, some fruits and nuts, etc. - items she was stealing anyway. Janie was then allowed to carry this with her wherever she went. More than allowed, Janie was encouraged and reminded to keep the backpack with her at all times. On more than one occasion Mrs. Noble would see Janie playing in the front yard without the backpack close by. When asked about it, Janie explained to her mother that the backpack was in the backyard. Not reassured by this, the foster mother instructed Janie to retrieve the backpack and to keep it close by at all times. Mrs. Noble explained, "You never know when hunger might strike!" The foster mother did this, of course, to assume a stronger role than Janie in worrying about food.

The backpack strategy was not used as a punishment, e.g. the pack was not loaded down with canned goods. Nor, was it employed as a form of public shaming of the child. It was explained to Janie that she needed and deserved to be fed and to be reassured that food was present and available. Likewise, she was told that her feelings were normal, given what she'd gone through in her life. The backpack was described as a way to remind Janie that her needs were important and would be met. She would not have to worry about it. With the foster mother taking on a lead role in worrying about the backpack and about constant availability of food for Janie, this child was eventually able to surrender her own preoccupation. Ironically, she reached a point where she told Mrs. Noble to not worry so much, "Don't worry about the backpack, Mom! I just had a big breakfast."

14. Fun-filled Eating

Some children have an impossible time sitting still at the table. Indeed, it is almost torturous for them to stay put while they eat. Others find the dinner table itself a negative experience. Not particularly interested in food, they much prefer playtime.

In one case, a four-year-old foster girl, Amy, refused to eat at the dinner table. The child seemed tense, stiff, and unsmiling when seated at the table. She alternately piddled with her food, wiggled and squirmed on the chair, and hunched over her plate staring morosely at the tiny portions which had been served up to her. The abuse history of this "unhappy diner" included deprivation, force feeding, and incidents of being lashed to the kitchen chair for hours to get her to eat.

Amy was observably fidgety, squirmy and plainly hyperactive at the table and, for that matter, in most areas of her life. Even TV failed to hold her attention for long. However, she could play with toys imaginatively for hours on end without interruption. She seemed to be considerably calm while assembling and disassembling puzzles, and manipulating snap together models, Legos, etc.

Observing this, Amy's experienced foster mother made a virtual playground out of the dinner table, rather than forbidding play and excess movement at the table. The food was served at the table, but no encouragement or cajoling was used. Almost absent-mindedly Amy began nibbling at her food while playing with the toys along with the foster mother who sometimes played with the child and ate simultaneously.

Instead of battling over compliance at the table, this foster mother took a different tack. Although we might not use this approach with all children (some of whom need to be sent from the table for misbehavior), this mother sized up what was needed and adapted to what the child could handle.

15. Midnight Snack at 3 A.M.

*J*unior was a highly compliant, superficially self-reliant, eight-year-old foster child. He rarely sought out help from his foster mother or father. While almost voyeuristic about watching other children receive hugs and affection from the foster parents, Junior, after twelve months in placement, seemed timidly withdrawn and non-initiating. The foster mother described him this way: *"He is a nervous little mouse around me...he sniffs at the cheese but never takes a bite."*

As a self-parenting child, Junior had learned many ways to nurture himself solitarily. Unused to care-giving from adults in his past, his modus operandi was to take care of his needs in secret. This extended even to the most basic of needs, such as food. Supper was especially noteworthy. At the family dinner table, Junior nibbled, dabbled and dawdled. While the other children insisted on several helpings, Junior seemed a bit overwhelmed by how public family dining really was. When the other children chattered excitedly to the foster parents and with each other about the day's activities, Junior was mum - quiet as a mouse.

Like a mouse, Junior was nocturnal. It was discovered that he awakened nightly at almost precisely three a.m. and quietly foraged for food while everyone else slept. At that hour of the night he could have all the privacy, quiet, and food he wanted without having to deal with other human beings in the process. It was an odd way of gathering sustenance, but it made sense in the context of his earlier exposure to neglect and abuse. Hunting and gathering of food was what helped this mouse-like little boy survive in the past. Unfortunately, the nocturnal acting-out stood in the way of new learning. It prevented Junior from reaching out to competent, nurturing parent figures.

When the foster parents discovered that Junior was a night feeder, they decided to address the issue without conflict or power-struggling with the child. Meeting him on familiar ground and then gently edging him to higher ground was their tactic. The foster parents alternated nights, setting their alarm clock for 2:30 a.m. The mother or father would gently wake Junior before 3 a.m. and carry him down to the kitchen, where a "midnight snack" was waiting. They often would spoon feed Junior while sitting him on their laps. After two months, Junior seemed more interested in sleeping through the night than in foraging for food. Indeed, when the foster parents awakened him in the *wee hours, Junior would mumble groggily that he was sleepy, cover his head with his covers, and go immediately back to sleep for the remainder of the night.*

10. My Voice Journeys with You

The human voice has tremendous soothing power. The voice of a loved one, or a trusted individual, can calm, strengthen, and soothe both adult and child. The next case description underscores how using the voice of one not physically present to the child can help the child through a difficult time:

Willie, age 10, had developed a close, reassuring bond to James, a staff member at the residential center, creating a doubled-edged sword. James' presence comforted and calmed Willie when he was on duty, but on days and nights when James was off, Willie was a basket case. He acted out with defiance and mulish stubbornness toward less preferred staff members. Willie's behavior was categorically different with James there.

At bedtime the problems worsened. Willie was inconsolable, agitated and manufactured crises which kept the center in an uproar. Sometimes it was necessary to call to James' house for a tete-a-tete with Willie by phone. When James was not there to read a story and tuck Willie into bed, the whole house paid dearly.

The central questions on the staff's minds were: "How can we better handle Willie when James is off duty?" "How could James continue to help Willie, even when he was not on duty?" "Could another staff member help?" (Unfortunately, Willie seemed comprehensively opposed to extending his trust and bond to other staff members.)

At a weekly clinical staff meeting, the consulting psychiatrist half-jokingly remarked, "Willie needs a security blanket at bedtime." Though some of the staff chortled, James took it more seriously, "I've been hoping to find a way to lessen Willie's dependence on me without rejecting him or sending him reeling. Another staff member added, "Maybe we could play music to him in the evening." Others suggested that since Willie loved his tape player and headphones, why not audiotape James' voice and let him listen to this as his falls off to sleep. A strategy was born!

Interestingly, the on-duty staff member who helped Willie find his head phones, and locate James' tape, eventually acquired a closer relationship to Willie. Thus, Willie now had two staff members who had a calming influence on him at bedtime. Now two voices had that comforting influence on Willie.

WORDS OF CAUTION ABOUT THE USE OF UNCONVENTIONAL STRATEGIES

As potentially beneficial as some unconventional strategies can be for reaching children, some words of caution are necessary here. In all instances, the best interests of the child must be paramount, when we employ any and all unorthodox interventions with them. The creativity or efficiency of the strategy does not justify the use of approaches which might in any way traumatize the child or send the child negative messages, as in the following case:

A residential treatment center staff was perplexed about how to handle the destructive rages of an eleven-year-old female resident. They braced themselves for the once per week explosive outbursts which routinely were set off by minor frustrations: e.g. when the staff limited Ginger, told her "no," or insisted that she complete her chores. She would predictably squabble, then fall silent and grow self-absorbed and glassy-eyed. Brief moments later she would sprint to her bedroom and proceed to demolish it violently. She shredded clothing, broke furniture, and left the room strewn with clothes, furniture, and miscellany. Then, just as suddenly as the outburst had begun, it was over—except, of course, for the massive clean-up which the staff required. Typically, Ginger would refuse to discuss the incident, her feelings, or what could be changed to make things turn out better.

The clinical supervisor of the residence suggested that when the silent, glassy-eyed behavior appeared, that the staff should race down the hallway ahead of Ginger and tear up her room for her. Prior to the next destructive spree, the staff, following orders, beat Ginger to the punch by charging down to her bedroom first, turning her room upside down, and smashing her dresser drawers to pieces. Interestingly, the residence never experienced another outburst from Ginger.

In reflecting on this strategy, it should be obvious that there are limits to the use of unconventional strategies. This is especially true when it comes to violent and sexual behaviors. Frightening, intimidating, and/or violent behavior cannot be condoned in the name of treatment. Though this intervention may have been innovative and effective, it did not appear humane. This intervention and others like it may model the escalation of aggressive behavior or other inappropriate actions.

A system of care has evolved which...contributes to a "system level" mistreatment of the very children it purports to help.

FIVE

Raising Cain with Our System

In our attempt to raise disturbed, abused children humanely and safely, a system of care has evolved which sometimes fails miserably. Indeed, on occasion it contributes to a system-level mistreatment of the very children it purports to help. This is not meant as an indictment of the many caring, dedicated, individual caseworkers, supervisors, administrators, and helping professionals who struggle daily to address the needs of troubled children living in care. However, serious questions must be directed at certain trends in our system, funding decisions, built-in structural flaws, and hackneyed procedures. Trends which fly in the face of what we know about children's needs, perceptions, and best interests. About that system we must "raise Cain."

This chapter will discuss serious concerns about the following areas:

1. The impact of managed care on foster and foster/adoptive children.

2. The goal of family preservation.

3. Forcing adoptions of extraordinary needs children.

4. The lack of specialized mental health services for foster and adoptive families.

5. Misguided practices in placement decisions.

1. Managed Care

While the managing of health care dollars is now firmly ensconced in most areas of the country, the domain of foster care has only recently been impacted. In the name of cutting costs and managing care more efficiently, we are now witnessing shorter lengths-of-stay in foster care; abridged stays in hospital and residential treatment settings; and expedited demotions of children from treatment foster care to regular foster care status.

Unbridled use of managed care may be inappropriate, if not outright dangerous for our most troubled and at-risk foster and adopted children. We must not compromise standards of safety for children in the name of cost-effectiveness. If we return children to birth families before the chronic maltreating conditions are remediated, we unconscionably endanger these youngsters. In that instance, managed care becomes damaged care.

Ironically, I believe that managed care may be the impetus that's needed to make certain overdue changes occur in our system of care. It has long been known that a scandalous number of children languish in foster care when the goal is to place them in adoptive homes. The delay, often three or more years, derives from the failure to terminate parental rights in a timely fashion. In some states, termination of parental rights is still a rarity, even when these parents have demonstrated the glaring incapacity to parent adequately. Even when these parents are deemed untreatable, parental rights remain intact. These drawn out, hopeless situations might actually benefit from the advent of managed care. The private sector which drives managed care will quickly deduce that it is quite costly keeping children in long-term foster care. Managed care will find a way to prompt quicker permanence for children, but for the wrong reason - money.

2. The Goal of Family Preservation

Family preservation services arise from a noble, virtually unassailable premise. Families should be preserved whenever reasonable and feasible. However, there is a precariousness to a wholesale endorsement of family preservation: the increased risk of trauma to and abuse of children. Accordingly, the family preservation impetus must be adequately counterbalanced by child protection efforts. Conversely, child protection efforts without the counter weight of family preservation produces overzealous placement of children out-of-home. While family preservation services are presently in vogue nationally, we should accurately assess which families should be and can be preserved as well as which should not and cannot be salvaged.

In many cases we have applied a plethora of services to families to shore them up, to preserve their integrity, and to allow them to parent their children. However, even when these families were provided extraordinary support, they remained unable to parent their children adequately. When props were entirely removed, the families were totally incapable of parenting their children safely. Though many of the caseworkers could have predicted that this "parenting by prosthesis" approach would fail, parents were given a chance to fail, fail again, and sometimes fail one more time, before removal of the children from situations antithetical to developing normally. In these instances, family preservation attempts persevered far too long.

Of course, it is impossible to be against family preservation as a general principle, as a central objective. But, the preservation of certain families is unconscionable. In many instances they are family "in name only."

3. Forcing Adoptions of Extraordinary Needs Children

Another nearly inarguable premise in our system is that "every child deserves a family." More specifically, the tenet is that children who have languished in foster care indefinitely deserve permanence, as in the permanence and security that an adoptive family can offer. Simply put, impermanence is the problem and adoption is the solution. Unfortunately, it is not always the solution. Sadly, forcing adoptions of some children can become part of the problem.

The Adoption and Safe Families Act signed by President Clinton in November, 1997, has been touted as a boon to children languishing in the foster care system. Its praiseworthy goals are to more expeditiously arrive at permanence for children, and to double the quota of children adopted each year by the year 2002. States will be reinforced with bounties of $4000 for each child adopted beyond a base line number and an extra $2000 incentive for each special needs child who is adopted. Now, while the emphasis on speeding permanency decisions for children is quite prudent and overdue, I am concerned that the proposed "quota and bounty" system may prompt abuses. More exactly, it may foster a myopic drivenness to perceive permanence as one thing, and only one thing - adoption. I suspect that when we get down to individual cases, we will see foster parents needlessly coerced to "adopt or drop" children who they have raised as their own for years. These foster parents may be threatened with removal of children for whom they have become psychological parents, unless they agree to adopt. In some instances foster parents are justifiably reluctant to adopt children without guarantees of long-term financial help for their special needs. These parents are willing to commit to the childrens' care, but understandably balk at the monetary burdens and liabilities that come with adopting.

Pressing families to adopt troubled children, without a full complement of financial and other supports in place, can result in increasing adoptive disruptions with accompanying trauma to both the adopted child and the family. The most realistic goal for the child in foster care should be the optimum permanence. In some instances this may be something other than the adoption option. Indeed, for some youngsters long-term, permanent foster care may be the acceptable, and sometimes superior choice. Furthermore, if the child is demonstrably family phobic, a caring group home placement may provide optimum permanence. (See "A Circle of Families" model in Chapter Six.)

Other concerns to be considered about adoptive placements are:

a. We sometimes unreasonably stretch prospective adoptive families beyond what they are initially prepared to take on. That is, if family 'X' approaches us about adopting an infant, we often give them an infant and two older, disturbed siblings as a package. When the family becomes attached to the infant, they are effectively blackmailed into keeping the troubled, disruptive siblings, lest they lose the infant.

b. We all too commonly prevent foster parents of a particular child from sharing information with the prospective adoptive parents, for fear that we might scare off the new family.

c. We fail to protect some zealous families from "adoption addiction." One overworked adoptive mother described the effects of her adoption addiction, "I found I could not say 'no' to adopting any child who needed a home. My birth children felt under-loved. My husband felt invisible. And yet, I could not stop myself - even after we had adopted our fifth child."

4. Lack of Specialized Mental Health Services for Foster & Adoptive Families

Mental health professionals potentially have much to contribute to the treatment team working with troubled foster and adoptive youngsters. However, it is essential to adapt mental health skills and approaches to the speciality area. Without close collaboration between the foster/adoptive parents, caseworkers and others impacting the child, mental health services can be meaningless at best and disruptive at worst. In the forefront of the mental health worker's view about this work should be the belief in the family as the essential change agent. Additionally, a sense of the importance of the family as both resource to and as a fund of knowledge about the child is equally as critical.

Unfortunately, feedback from foster and adoptive parents is not universally positive about mental health involvement. Indeed, comments from foster and adoptive parents suggest that many mental health professionals are out of sync with the basic needs of the foster and adoptive family as well as the child. Foster parents and adoptive parents around the country attest that they often seek advice from mental health professionals about managing their foster or adopted child, but come away frustrated. They state that dogmatic, black-and-white advice is not appreciated. Nor, is a total dearth of suggestions from the mental health professional.

Non-directive psychotherapy is commonly unpopular with foster and adoptive parents who frequently cannot identify improvements in their child related to that mental health approach. Many parents fail to receive explanations from the therapist about what positive (or negative) changes to expect. Many disgruntled foster and adoptive parents have felt that the children did not have to deal with the real, painful issues in nondirective therapies. They felt that there seemed to be no "ending point" for therapy. Thus, the parents' sense was that therapy is well-intentioned but aimless and endless. They feel they are left to deal with the child's difficult problems and challenging behaviors, while therapy is "fun and games."

According to foster and adoptive parents, mental health services occurring in a vacuum, without tie-in to the family, can promote splitting, disruptiveness in the home, irrelevance of the psychotherapy, and general ineffectiveness. Foster and adoptive parents voice concerns about children who may lie to the therapist or be on best behavior in the therapy sessions, giving the therapist a skewed picture of the true child. Some foster parents feel devalued and excluded by the insular approach of many mental health professionals. Still other foster and adoptive parents are understandably alarmed about the therapist who aligns with their child without input from them. In some situations this may result in the therapist taking on an adversarial role toward the parents.

Confidentiality between therapist and child sometimes feels counterproductive and senseless to foster and adoptive parents. It often leaves them feeling in the dark, defensive, and disempowered. It appears that a rigid adherence to confidentiality, even with children of tender years, can promote a sense of isolation and even wariness in foster and adoptive parents. (Given the notion that with many of today's disturbed foster and adopted children we have a "psychiatric children's hospital without walls," the rules of confidentiality may need to be altered dramatically. For, in what psychiatric hospital do staff members refuse to discuss clinical details with each other?)

Many foster and adoptive parents report "magical" changes when their child is prescribed on the right medication for depression, ADHD, bi-polar disorder, etc. However, other foster and adoptive parents are alarmed by how little time was spent with their child before medication was prescribed. These parents see cursory medical assessments which end with almost knee-jerk prescriptions of Ritalin, Prosac, Lithium, and the like. (Note: Parents are not alone in their concerns about medication of children. Psychologists have voiced strong concerns about a rampant, "Better Living Through Chemistry," approach to dealing with children's emotional/behavioral problems.)

Although exceptions exist, many foster and adoptive parents are dissatisfied with mental health services for their disturbed children. They feel disempowered, discredited, excluded, and sometimes incriminated and blamed by mental health professionals who treat their children. They feel the children are coddled but rarely confronted by therapists. The therapists then leave them - the parents - to deal with the child's difficult problems in the home. In general, foster and adoptive parents do not feel included as part of the treatment team. Unfortunately, they do not often encounter therapists who have specific knowledge about the specialty of fostering and adopting troubled children. Moreover, they rarely find therapists who have embraced the orientation necessary to work within the "psychiatric children's hospital without walls."

5. Misguided Practices in Placement Decisions

In our search to ensure permanency for all children, we often make placement decisions which are misguided, as in the following case:

A teenaged girl with a history of multiple foster and adoptive placements, had lived comfortably in a group home for two years. This was the longest, uninterrupted period of time she had been in one placement in her life. The school system, impressed by the girl's academic performance and successful participation in sports, felt that she deserved better than group home care. Additionally, neighbors, befriended by this girl, came forward and petitioned the court to allow them to adopt her. Ignoring the caseworker's opinion that the girl was family phobic and would likely sabotage the adoption, the court directed that the youth be placed with the prospective adoptive parents. A week before the placement was to occur, however, the girl was caught shoplifting on several occasions. Her previously controlled temper erupted, she became verbally and physically abusive to classmates and was expelled. Her group home placement, without daily school attendance, became more stressful for her. Behavior problems, accordingly escalated, and the teen was ultimately hospitalized after a suicide attempt.

About the above-described case (and with the obvious luxury of hindsight), we might ask, "Was the adoption attempt well-advised? Did we define permanency too myopically? Should we have left well enough alone?" In this unfortunate case, we sacrificed continuity of care for the vision of a superior form of permanence. Placement decisions of all sorts must reflect sensitivity to the individual case and specific child. Placements based on platitudes and generalizations are devoid of common sense and short-change foster and adopted children.

SIX

Raising Cain Better

Admittedly, our present system of care has major structural flaws, such as gla-cially plodding procedures for moving children toward permanence and glaring defects in support for foster and adoptive parents. However, those faults are reparable. Moreover, those of us entrusted with the multi-faceted process of care-giving for our troubled foster and adopted children **can** alter the system. We can, for example, expedite court decisions which move children to permanency. This could decrease the amount of foster care drift and impermanence which compromises the ability to attach. Additionally, we can make prudent, common sense placement decisions which reflect a sensitivity to the needs of the child. We can develop innovative programs which recognize the worsening level of distur-bance in foster and foster/adoptive children; the specialized training which parents will require to deal with the challenges; and the prevalence of children with family phobia (which undermines their capacity to accept conventional family life). Fur-ther, by the use of well organized parent support groups, we can more effectively harness the collective wisdom of talented, knowledgeable foster and adoptive parents to improve placement stability and to increase successful outcomes. Lastly, using what we know about the importance of rest and recuperation for foster and adoptive parents, we can develop innovative respite care which insures place-ment stability.

In this final chapter we will discuss positive trends, policies, programs, and proce-dures which will help us to raise Cain better. These are the following:

1. Concurrent planning.

2. Twelve factors to weigh in placement decisions.

3. Circle of families model.

4. The collective wisdom of parent support groups.

5. Respite care.

1. Concurrent Planning

The problem of children in limbo - children languishing in the foster care system, drifting through multiple placements over the years - was addressed but not solved by the Adoption Assistance and Child Welfare Act of 1980. To this day in many states, foster children are subjected to unbearably long waits, while the legal/welfare system grinds to its conclusion about permanency, as in the following case:

The Jones family first came to the attention of the county child protection team in 1988. Mrs. Jones was an unemployed, substance abusing, overwhelmed mother of four school-aged children. She was provided with homemaker support, parenting classes, and a drug and alcohol evaluation. Day care was provided for the children, as well as psychotherapy for mother. With all props in place the family seemed to tread water, through "parenting by prosthesis." Unfortunately, when Mrs. Jones was weaned off the supports even partially, her neglectful, abusive approach re-emerged. Even during the most intensive periods of support, she continued to abuse alcohol. Periodically, when her own personal instability became most problematic, Mrs. Jones would request foster care for her children. At other times the department would remove the children on its own initiative. After six years and multiple foster home placements, more aggressive efforts were made to find permanence for the four children. By this time they were all showing major emotional and behavioral problems. Termination of parental rights was sought and granted but only after three years of courtroom wrangling, delays, and appeals. By the time the children were legally free for adoption, in 1997, they were essentially unadoptable due to age and severity of emotional problems - both direct results of prolonging the inevitable. In retrospect workers felt that they should have sought for termination earlier.

In answer to the problems seen in the Jones' case, an experimental model is currently under study in numerous states across the country. (With the November, 1997 enactment of The Adoption & Safe Families Act, states are scrambling to comply with requirements of expedited permanency for children.) The new model, i.e. concurrent planning, offers guidelines crucial for achieving timely permanence for children, by means of (A) termination of parental rights and placement of the child for adoption; or (B) reunification of the child with birth family members. In this model (see Katz, 1993), as a child comes into out-of-home care due to maltreatment, the following steps are taken:

1. The caseworker completes an evaluation of the family, pinpointing the problems which will jeopardize or prevent reunification, if they remain unchanged.

2. Within two months relatives are contacted as possible placement setting for the child/children. Legal fathers are identified. Applicability of the Indian Child Welfare Act is determined.

3. An explicit recounting of the results of the assessment are shared with the family, family attorney, the child's attorney and others. A written service plan is developed to address central problems. Concurrent planning is explained to the parents with specific descriptions of Permanency Plans A and B. Plan A is reunification. Plan B is relinquishment or termination of parental rights which would free the child for adoption.

4. A visitation schedule is developed based upon the child's needs for access to the birth family.

5. If the assessment has determined that reunification is unlikely, the options of foster/adoptive or kinship placement are openly discussed with the birth parents. Relinquishment of parental rights is explored.

6. If no progress has been made within 90 days after the service plan is in place, the caseworker initiates Plan B.

Concurrent planning emphasizes front loading of assessment to determine what problems need to be addressed. It also attempts to determine expeditiously the prognosis for reunification of parents and child. This approach avoids prejudging families or withholding services from high risk families. At the same time, it attempts to spot "un-treatable" parents as early as possible. The thrust of concurrent planning is to arrive at timely permanence for children, to reduce length of stay in foster care, and to reduce foster care drift (cf. Katz, 1993).

Although concurrent planning offers more expedient, humane planning for the child, some problems may arise related to the foster/adoptive placement. Specifically, if we send a child directly to a foster/adoptive home without a thorough assessment of his/her emotional and behavioral problems this may preclude proper matching with an appropriate foster/adoptive home. Foster/adoptive families may encounter problems which only emerge after placement has surpassed the honeymoon stage. Once the true extent of the child's problems have been revealed, some families may be unwilling to adopt. Especially with first time foster/adoptive families, we may risk a disrupted placement once the child's previously unobserved problems surface.

*If needed, can relatives protect the child from the birth parents'
disruptive incursions?*

2. Twelve Factors to Weigh in Placement Decisions

Baby Jessica De Boeur, Baby Richard, Baby XYZ - all seen in the headlines. News papers were full of stories about placement indecencies foisted upon them. The public was outraged, laws were passed and promises were made. We will not allow this mindless maltreatment of children by the system to reoccur! Nonetheless, the same placement decisions made for Jessica are occurring all across the country.

Consider what we know about child psychology, about the child's perception of time, and about the fragility of the young psyche. Yet we continually subject youngsters to unconscionably misguided decisions about their lives, especially about with whom they will live. Despite what we know about their attachment to others and how it must be protected, placement decisions often reduce children to chattel, as in the following case:

A widowed, sixty-something foster mother approached me recently to testify in court on behalf of her two foster children. The girls, ages 5 and 4, had been removed abruptly from her care to be adopted by strangers. Though this foster mother had raised both children for almost four uninterrupted years, the system had determined that there was a better home for them. The heart-broken foster parent had made it clear all along that she would adopt the children, to whom she was "Mom." Clearly, she was the children's psychological parent, the only care-giver they knew.

Somehow, the county department of social services determined that the girls would go, due to the age of the foster mother, with a younger family. The foster parent, knowing she had no legal standing in court in that state, reluctantly resigned herself to the grim fact that she would lose the children. Only the promise of an open adoption, which would permit on-going visits, offered any consolation.

Unfortunately, the foster mother never received visits with her foster daughters, who were extremely distressed about leaving "Mom." The promise of visits was not legally binding, but purely at the discretion of the adoptive parents, who underestimated the importance of continuity of contact between their newly adopted daughters and the girl's psychological parent.

The quest to protect children from maltreatment only begins with removal from the immediate circumstances of harm. Placement decisions made once the children are in protective custody can reduce or increase trauma to children. To eliminate or, at the least, mitigate the trauma which our own system of care inadvertently inflicts upon children, we might consider the following twelve factors:

a. Child's Attachment Hierarchy

It is essential to determine to whom the child is attached. Who do they look to for security and protection? Who have they connected with psychologically? What is the hierarchy of attachments, i.e. which attachments are most significant, and how are attachments to important individuals ranked? Additionally, what is the nature of attachments to these individuals? Specifically, if we are considering splitting a sibling group, what is the nature of the attachment among these children? How does it compare with the attachments between the children and their foster/adoptive parents?

b. Protection of Continuity of Care/Permanence

In which ultimate placement would the child experience the most continuity of care? How would the child's life be least disrupted? Emotionally, what would present the least turmoil, confusion, trauma, and anxiety? From which individuals, adult or child, would the child experience the greatest separation anxiety and abandonment fears?

c. Best Interests of the Child

What placement serves the child's best interests? The best interests would include the physical health, safety and well-being; the emotional and psychological needs of the child; and the promotion of eventual self-sufficiency. What are the child's preferences about whom they would live with?

d. Least Detrimental Alternative

Which placement option for the child contains the least harm, potential or actual? If all options have intrinsic deficits or negative impact, which of the options has fewer harmful or deleterious effects?

e. Recognition of Psychological Parenthood

Who does the child view as his/her parents? Who are the observable, de facto parent figures to the child? To whom does the child feel he/she belongs? Which house is experienced and perceived as home?

f. Access to Ancillary Attachment Figures

In which placement setting do the adults appreciate the need for the child to have access to and contact with past and present attachment figures? If a separation of siblings is contemplated, do the care-givers commit to sibling contact, if it could mitigate damage to existing attachments among and between the children?

g. Parental Capacity

What are the parenting capacities and skills of the available homes? Do the parent figures have "good enough" parenting abilities to adequately parent the child? Are there any situational factors which might limit or augment the parent's capacity to raise a child?

h. Needs of Other Children

Are there children already living in the foster or adoptive home, whose needs would be severely compromised or sacrificed by on-going placement of another child or other children in the home? Are we reasonably certain that the current adjustment of children already in the home will not be destabilized or jeopardized by new arrivals?

i. King Solomon's Rule

Which of the available parent figures has the deepest concern for and understanding of the needs of the child to be placed? Which parents seem to be most cognizant of the child's developmental needs? Which are most protective of the child's basic well-being?

j. Least Restrictive Environment

If we are considering a range of placement options for a troubled child, we must look for the least restrictive setting. If the child could function well in a therapeutic foster home, he should not be living in a residential treatment center long-term. If he is adoptable, he should not be residing in a group home. We want the child to be placed in the most humane, family or family-like setting possible.

k. Kinship Care

Are birth relatives available to take this child into their home? If so, what is their level of functioning and capacity to parent. Have they had an important attachment relationship to this child and vice versa? If needed can the relatives protect the child from the birth parents' disruptive incursions?

l. Cultural Issues

If the child is from a minority group, can the child immediately be placed in a family of the same or similar culture? It is harmful to foster children if they are placed with a good home, only to be removed later because of racial mismatching.

When it comes to the placement of children, we are not conducting a beauty contest. Hypothetically, there might always be a better family - a younger family, in our case above - for the child or children. Ironically, though we might locate an extraordinarily talented family for a given child, it may be reckless and inhumane to place that specific child with them, if the child is already living with a "good enough" family to whom he/she is attached. In the unfortunate scenario described above, psychological parenthood, attachment, and continuity of care should have taken precedence over who is the "better" family. When a child is already attached, has feelings of belonging, and experiences security in one home, there must be compelling justification to move him/her. Indeed, I believe that the criteria for uprooting the child who is secure in his current foster or adoptive home should be as stringent as the criteria met in the initial removal due to child maltreatment.

Hopefully, keeping in mind the dozen factors related above, we can reduce the chances of insensitive decision making and resultant system-generated damage to children.

3. A Circle Of Families

When it comes to treating disturbed foster and adopted children, we are always searching for a better mouse trap. Indeed, with the caliber of disturbance found in today's "psychiatric children's hospital without walls," better inventions are a must. One program, still in its inception, is "Circle Of Families" (COF). This program is designed to meet the needs of seriously emotionally troubled children and adolescents in a non-institutional setting. COF takes the best of what a traditional foster or adoptive family provides any child: care, nurturing, guidance, love, belonging, and permanence. At the same time COF brings together a group of well-trained, well-supported professional parents who operate in a concerted, coordinated way to provide a community, a protective circle for the children to grow up in.

COF builds upon the notion of families collectively sharing the raising of seriously disturbed children and adolescents. The underlying tenet of COF is that often times one family is not enough to take on extremely disturbed youngsters, especially as they exit residential, institutional, and hospital settings to reside in the community. Additionally, when children are truly "family phobic," they often drift from one destroyed foster placement to another. They can convince first time or even seasoned parents to take an early retirement from fostering. These children reside in many homes over time and experience multiple placements sequentially, because they cannot tolerate the intimacy and intensity of life in one family.

Problems Addressed:

The Circle Of Families project plans to address eight interrelated issues concerning the care and treatment of seriously disturbed children:

a. It will allow for the cost-effective treatment of disturbed children and adolescents, previously only workable in inpatient settings. Two or more families working collectively will raise children who otherwise would sequentially amass numbers of disrupted placements.

b. It will allow for the successful, plan-full, and correct matching of families with children.

c. It will provide new foster parents with "on the job training" in a receiving/ shelter (RS) home, through which all children will pass on their way to individual home placements.

d. It will involve the part-time staffing of the RS home by the foster parents themselves, who will come and go from their own homes, as well as full-time staffing by group home parents residing in the RS facility.

e. It will offer shelter to children entering the program. These children will receive screening and evaluation by the foster parents and other professionals. A central component of the program will be heavy involvement of foster parents in the assessment of the children and in decisions about placement.

f. It will focus upon respite services which truly support the child, the foster parents, and the stability of placements.

g. It will offer as permanent and family-like a setting as possible for all children entering the program. In some instances, this may involve raising the child by "tag team parenting." Additionally, it will allow for the proactive, temporary movement of a child from one COF home to another (and then, later, back again to that home). These decisions will be made by the program staff and team of parents raising that child.

h. It will address the issue of crisis intervention by providing respite services offered by surrogate grandparents, who will also handle much of the day-to-day support of individual families and children. Crisis programming will also be part of the RS home.

Program Schematic:

The program schematic (see next page) illustrates the structure of the COF. The circle represents the RS home which will be staffed by a live-in couple with additional part-time staffing provided by the foster parents clustered around it. The four pentagons represent the individual foster homes. The rectangles represent the surrogate grandparents. The RS home, at the core, provides the ultimate backstop for children in crisis. Overall, it acts as the intake or admission center; the diagnostic facility; the shelter, crisis or respite center; as well as the training facility for new foster parents entering the program.

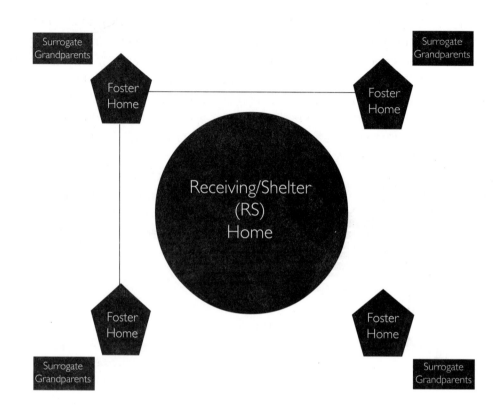

Family Phobic Youngsters:

One of the biggest challenges faced by our system of care today is the child or adolescent who is family phobic. This child has often been multiply placed. He/she is a foster care drifter who actively torpedoes permanency and intimacy of family life. Foster care programs across the country all struggle with this child, who formerly was referred to as institutionalized. This is the child who "blows out" of regular foster homes, therapeutic foster homes, and yet does well in group homes, residential treatment centers, or in hospital or state institutions. When this child seems to thrive in institutional settings, we inevitably attempt to place them within a foster or adoptive family. To our chagrin, the child fails miserably in the family setting. These are the children who may be nearly impossible to raise in a single family. The inherent risk of intimate living is too great for these youngsters. To them, "family" is a dirty word.

We need new models to address the family phobic child - models which reflect our understanding of the dynamics of drift, the intricacies of intimacy phobia. The Circle Of Families will allow for tailoring the permanency and intimacy of family living to each individual child. We anticipate that many of the children coming through the RS home will successfully connect with and reside with an individual family. However, some children will balk, evade, or sabotage attempts to place them permanently with one family. For these children the COF will allow for tag team parenting in which the child might be raised by a "therapeutic kibbutz" of two or more foster families which will plan-fully share the parenting of the child between and among their homes. This will permit for a kind of respite for the families in cases where the child's behavior is overwhelming and exhausting, or in situations wherein the child needs to dilute intimacy. When families detect that the child's behavior is about to escalate, they may defuse the situation by a therapeutic move to another member in the circle.

Other Salient Program Features:

• Surrogate grandparents will provide the "extended family" for both the children and the foster parents. They will act as mentors, trainers, confidants, advisors, and assistants.

• COF will solicit a Guardian-Ad-Litem or CASA (Court Appointed Special Advocate) volunteer for each child admitted to the program.

• Training of new foster parents will occur in the RS home under the direct supervision of the house foster parents and other COF parents. The training will permit for a certification of parents as "professional parents."

• Psychological, psychiatric, and other ancillary services will be provided on a contract basis.

A COF presupposes that participating families understand that this is a group effort, tag-teaming of a child, and that no one owns the child exclusively. Trust, cooperation and open communication are essential for a shared parenting project to work. Territoriality, competition, and secrecy are destructive to successful conjoint care of a troubled child.

It is important to note here that some COF foster children may eventually become adoptable while in the program, e.g. not only legally free for adoption but also psychologically capable of handling it. For the sake of continuity and to protect attachment, a member, or members of the child's tag team of parents would be considered first, if adoption becomes a realistic option for the child.

Potential Impediments to Establishing Circle Of Families Model:

Although the COF model has much to commend it, there are at least two potential impediments to it's implementation:

   a. Recruitment and selection of families who are willing to enter a therapeutic kibbutzim model. The mental set of families contemplating or already engaged in foster care work does not typically include the notion of conjoint parenting.

   b. Agency caseworkers may initially hesitate to place children within the COF due to a concern about denying the child a normal, one-family-one-child placement. There can be justifiable worry about failing to allow the child the opportunity to develop a sense of truly belonging to a family.

Comments:

Given the level of disturbance now prevalent in children in care, we must develop innovative approaches to stabilize placements and to decrease frequency of drifting. COF is one planned innovation which might reach children who previously could only be stabilized in residential facilities.

4. Collective Wisdom of Parent Staffing Groups

Research on foster and adoptive care has shown that two resources help save placements: (a) readily available respite care (cf. subsection five ahead) and (b) parent support and staffing groups. Parent staffing groups in particular offer an invaluable source of support and advice for foster and adoptive parents. As most foster and adoptive parents eventually realize over time, few individuals understand what they experience with their troubled child. What's more, mental health professionals and agency workers sometimes are unable to give foster and adoptive parents clear, helpful ideas and directions for these youngsters. A feeling of unreality befalls many foster and adoptive parents when they find themselves looked upon suspiciously by professionals, who often reflexively align with the disturbed child's distorted perceptions of the family. To make matters worse, foster and adoptive parents are typically misunderstood by their own extended families, friends, neighbors, and co-workers who think they understand better how to raise a child. Sometimes with the best of intentions these individuals offer free advice which reflects their own view of children - mostly normal children. While most of these individuals may be sincerely attempting to help, it may not be felt as such by the foster or adoptive family, which begins to realize how poorly others really understand. Unfortunately, things can go from bad to worse as family members, friends, and neighbors become increasingly judgmental toward the foster or adoptive parents, blaming them for the child's continuing emotional problems.

The value of parent support and staffing groups is in its collective wisdom and in the intuitive understanding shared among members. It becomes evident that this cadre of parents really understands what its members are going through, because they have been there too. It is rare when someone in the group has not already experienced problems with their child similar to those raised by another member, as seen in the following case:

Mrs. Britta, a beleaguered foster mother, felt that she was the problem. So did her mother-in-law and so did her husband. Bobby, a conniving eleven-year-old, male, foster child had skillfully "conned" Grandma and the foster father into believing that the mother was cruel to him. Outside of their view he acted up with the foster mother, meanwhile treating them to a very agreeable facade. Mrs. Britta's description of her daytime struggles with Bobby, his lying, physical threats to her, and foul mouth, seemed unbelievable to the other adults around her. Indeed, Mr. Britta began to have serious doubts about his wife. Obviously, a chasm yawned between them. Interestingly, as Mrs. Britta grew more negative and punitive with Bobby, Mr. Britta countered with more lenience. With that, the polarization of discipline increased.

Luckily, the Britta's began attending a foster parent support group in a last ditch effort to turn things around in their home. Almost immediately, the foster mothers in the support group spotted the "textbook" dynamic. Mrs. Britta had become the "scape-Mom," while her husband had become the unwitting patsy. When several foster fathers in the group confessed that they had previously found themselves at odds with their wives over their troubled children, Mr. Britta began to listen.

Gradually, the support of Mrs. Britta by the group members (and eventually, by her husband) turned the tide for the family. Additionally it reassured Mrs. Britta that she was not going crazy. Mr. Britta, on the advice of the other foster fathers, took on more of a disciplinarian role with Bobby. This action relieved Mrs. Britta of her thankless job with Bobby. Further, it permitted Mr. Britta the chance to see a different side of Bobby; one he had previously reserved for Mrs. Britta alone.

As the anecdote shows, parent support groups can impart a great deal to their members. Such groups understand the dynamics of other foster and adoptive families. They know what importing a troubled child into the home can do to the relationships therein. Also, group members realize that conventional parenting approaches and techniques fall short with disturbed foster and adopted children. They know the toll which raising a troubled youngster can take on members of the family, the marriage and their physical and mental well-being. Importantly, they intuitively empathize with other foster and adoptive parents who ventilate their feelings of frustration. They can permit each other the much needed opportunity to vocalize those painful sentiments without becoming appalled or critical.

The upshot here is that foster and adoptive placements which are supported via parent groups last longer. In counties and states where a system of support groups is available, placements survive and thrive. Foster and adoptive parents feel less isolated, less burned out, and more willing to continue with current placements.

5. Respite Care: The Pause that Refreshes

Respite care can make a significant difference in success of placements. Successful foster and adoptive programs place strong emphasis on supporting their families post-placement. One chief avenue of support is to provide relief from continuous care-giving through respite.

Clinical experience shows that both foster and adoptive parents who are raising troubled children benefit from periodic, short-term breaks provided by respite care. Respite care can be as short as one evening in length or as long as a week or month. It can be used pro-actively to prevent the build up of tension and exhaustion in the parents. It can be used in situations where an immediate, emergency period of separation from the child is needed. Unfortunately, many foster and adoptive parents have no access to respite homes.

While it is evident that both foster and adoptive parents function better when intermittent rest, relaxation and relief are provided, there are other benefits from respite care which we often overlook. It is easy to see the secondary benefits to the foster or adoptive child. His care-givers feel better, they parent more effectively and the child is the beneficiary. However, the direct benefits of respite care to the child are sometimes more difficult to imagine. One central benefit derives from the new found perspective the child receives when placed away from the home. Perhaps, a few words about what we mean by perspective would be in order here. But, first an example of a child placed into respite care.

Charles was a fourteen-year-old adopted boy who frequently acted oppositional, rebellious, and defiant towards his parents. He often assumed the attitude that his adoptive parents, who had adopted him at ten, had no right to discipline him or to tell him what to do. Charles typically back-talked his parents, muttered mutinous thoughts under his breath, and at other times simply turned his back on them and walked away in the middle of discussions. "You are not my parents!" was his oft-spoken remark.

Returning to their adoptive caseworker, Mr. and Mrs. Toppler, Charles' adoptive parents, appeared quite frazzled and perplexed. They felt ill-prepared to deal with the anger which Charles directed at them. While they were able to maintain a certain fragile composure with him during even his most unpleasant exchanges, the Topplers gener-

ally felt bewildered, exasperated, and out of ideas. They were, by their own admission, near the end of the proverbial rope.

The caseworker quickly perceived how jeopardized the adoptive placement was. Talking with the boy and his psychotherapist, and later meeting with Charles and Mr. and Mrs. Toppler, she sensed that a brief placement in a respite home might calm things down. Interestingly, it did much more than that. Mr. and Mrs. Toppler not only felt better after a re-fueling break from Charles, but Charles himself returned to the Toppler home with a new attitude. Charles had a more cooperative spirit and a new found perspective about his adoptive parents. He realized that they had a limit to what they would put up with from him. The Topplers became more credible in his eyes, because "they actually did it...sent me off to cool my heels." (Charles seemed oddly relieved that they would finally put their foot down.) Secondly, Charles had been sent to a respite home that was experienced and savvy. The parents (former therapeutic foster parents) played the role of tough, disciplinarian parents. When Charles experienced how strict, firm, and no-nonsense this respite household was, he couldn't wait to get back to his adoptive parents!

Unfortunately, when children and adolescents leave foster or adoptive homes for a stay in respite care, they do not always return with an improved openness to and appreciation of their families. In fact, if the respite home is too lenient, too attentive, or too indulgent, the youngsters can return with a worsened attitude. In these instances, they tend to idealize the respite home which may only amplify the devaluation of their foster or adoptive family. It is important for caseworkers and therapists to select and monitor very carefully the respite homes which are used to assist beleaguered foster and adoptive parents. Wherever possible, respite homes should be specially trained and experienced in this role. Additionally, the respite parents must agree to be supportive of the foster or adoptive parents by not inadvertently spoiling the child. With a youngster like Charles, for example, the most helpful respite experience would be structured, firm and matter of fact. Contrariwise, the respite home which would make the stay a Disneyland experience (e.g. without responsibility, without discipline), might indirectly undermine the child's ability to better appreciate his foster or adoptive family. This is not to suggest that the respite experience needs to be harsh or cold. It should provide safety and concern for the child, albeit without an attempt to assume a parent role.

Whether respite care serves to refresh parents or to realign the child's thinking, longevity of the placement often depends upon it.

Afterward

A recent U.S. poll found almost universal, positive support for the concept of adoption. However, when asked more specific questions, those polled harbored "misgivings" about adoption. (With media exposure and television talk show coverage of adoptions-gone-bad, it is a wonder that we have any individuals willing to take on the risk of adopting - and especially adopting the older, special needs child.) A national shortage of foster parents may signal how widespread these misgivings have become about opening hearth, home and hearts to troubled children, foster or adopted. Interestingly, The Child Welfare League of America, the David and Lucille Packard Foundation, The Casey Family Program, and the Annie E. Casey Foundation have jointly launched the "Take This Heart" campaign to increase awareness nationwide about the need for foster care. Hopefully, with this effort, there will emerge an increase in successful recruitment of dedicated foster parents. (Once recruited, of course, these foster parents will require post-placement support to ensure successful outcomes with their troubled youngsters.)

With President Clinton's stated goal of doubling adoptions by the year 2002, we have our work cut out for us.* The spirit of giving must overcome the specter of misgivings. The risks inherent in adopting a special needs child must be disclosed openly, but also addressed thoroughly through supportive post-adoption services.

It is hoped that Raising Cain will help provide some assistance to foster and adoptive parents, caseworkers, mental health professionals, and other helpers in their work with troubled foster and adopted children. This cadre of care-givers must cope within an admittedly flawed system of care, while doggedly redesigning better ways to raise Cain.

* (Note: 100,000 children are available for adoption nationally, yet only 25% of them are adopted yearly.)

References and Recommended Reading

Adoption Assistance and Child Welfare Act of 1980. Public Law 96-272. U.S. Statutes at Large, 94, Part I. Washington, D.C.: U.S. Government Printing Office.

Adoption and Safe Families Act of 1997. Public Law 105-89. U.S. Statutes at Large. Washington, D.C.: U.S. Government Printing Office.

American Psychological Association Monitor. The Cherrypicking of Treatment Research. Washington, D.C.: American Psychological Association, Volume 29, Number 12, 1997.

American Psychological Association Monitor. Are Children Being Overmedicated? Washington, D.C.: American Psychological Association, Volume 29, Number 12, 1997.

American Psychological Association Monitor. Foster Children Get A Taste Of Stability. Washington, D.C.: American Psychological Association, June, 1997.

Baker, Christina B.; Burke, Ray V.; Herron, Ron W.; Mott, Mariam A., Rebuilding Childrens' Lives: A Blueprint for Treatment Foster Parents. Boy's Town, Nebraska: BT Press, 1996.

Barth, Richard P. Social and Cognitive Treatment of Children and Adolescents. San Francisco: Jossey-Bass, 1988.

Bettleheim, Bruno. The Uses of Enchantment: The Meaning and Importance of Fairy Tales. New York: Random House, 1975.

Brethauer, S. and Westfall, T. It Shouldn t Hurt To Be A Child. Idalia, Colorado: Rustic Realm Publication, 1995.

Brodzinsky, D.M., Schechter, M.D., and Henig, R. M. Being Adopted: The Lifelong Search for Self. New York, N.Y.: Doubleday, 1992.

Chamberlain, P. and Reid, John B. Using A Specialized Foster Care Community Treatment Model for Children and Adolescents Leaving the State Mental Hospital, Journal of Community Psychology, Volume 19, July, 1991.

Child Welfare League of America. Standards of Excellence for Family Foster Care Services. Washington, D.C.: CWLA, 1995.

Child Welfare League of America. Take This Heart: National Foster Care Awareness Project. Washington, D.C.: CWLA, 1997.

Delaney, Richard J. Fostering Changes: Treating Attachment-Disordered Foster Children. Fort Collins, CO: Walter J. Corbett Publishing, 1991.

Delaney, Richard J. The Long Journey Home. Oklahoma City, OK: Wood N. Barnes Publishing, 1994.

Delaney, Richard J. and Kunstal, Frank R. Troubled Transplants: Unconventional Strategies for Helping Disturbed Foster and Adopted Children. Oklahoma City, OK: Wood N. Barnes Publishing, 1993.

Division of Child and Family Services. Department of Public Health and Human Services. State of Montana. Foster Home Licensing Requirements. (Revised.) April, 1996.

Donley, Kathryn S. and Haimes, Rochelle. Further Dimensions in Child Placement: Current Practice in Residential Group Care and Adoption Collaboration. Southfield, Michigan: Spaulding for Children, 1992.

Emenhiser, D.; Barker, R.; DeWoody, M. Managed Care: An Agency Guide to Surviving and Thriving. Washington, D.C.: Child Welfare League of America, 1995.

Fahlberg, Vera I. A Child s Journey Through Placement. Indianapolis, IN: Perspectives Press, 1991.

Fanshel, David, Finch, Stephen J., and Grundy, John F. Foster Children in a Life Course Perspective. New York, NY: Columbia University Press, 1990.

Feild, Tracey. Managed Care and Child Welfare—Will It Work? Public Welfare, Summer, 1996.

Gelles, Richard J. Family Reunification Versus Child Protection. The Brown University Child and Adolescent Behavior Letter, Vol. 8, No.5, June, 1992.

Gore, Catherine A. The Long-Term Network Program Report. Cincinatti, OH: New Life Youth Services, 1993.

James, Beverly. Handbook for Treatment of Attachment-Trauma Problems in Children. New York, NY: Macmillan, 1994.

Kadushin, Alfred. Adopting Older Children. New York: Columbia University Press, 1970.

Kunstal, Frank R., Personal Communication, 1997.

Katz, Linda; Spoonemore, N.; Robinson, C. Concurrent Planning: From Permanency Planning to Permanency Action, Lutheran Family Services of Washington, 1994.

McKenzie, Judith K. Adoption of Children With Special Needs, in The Future of Children. Los Altos, CA: The Center for the Future of Children, 1993.

McNamara, Joan and McNamara, Bernard H. (Editors.) Adoption and the Sexually Abused Child. Portland, ME: University of Southern Maine, 1990.

Melina, Lois. Raising Adopted Children. New York, N.Y.: Solstice Press, 1986.

Melina, Lois. Public Divided In Attitudes Towards Adoption. The Adopted Child. Volume 16, Number 12, December, 1997.

Moustakas, Clark E. Psychotherapy with Children. Greeley, CO: Carron Publishers, 1959.

Nelson, Krista. Fostering Homeless Children and Their Parents Too: The Emergence of Whole-Family Foster Care. Child Welfare League of America. Washington, D.C.: CWLA, Vol. LXXI, Number 6, 1992.

North American Council on Adoptable Children. The Adoption Assistance and Child Welfare Act of 1980 (Public Law 96-272): The First Ten Years. St. Paul, Minnesota: NACAC, 1990.

Rosenthal, James A. Outcomes of Adoption of Children with Special Needs, in The Future of Children. Los Altos, CA: The Center for the Future of Children, 1993.

Schene, Patricia. Expedited Permanency Planning In Colorado. Denver, CO: Colorado Department of Human Services, 1996.

Sittenfield-Battistello, Ellen. Making Managed Health Care Work For Kids in Foster Care: A Guide To Purchasing Services. Washington, D.C.: CWLA Press, 1996.

Sobraske, John. Building A Camp-Based Respite Program For Adopted and Foster Youth. Minneapolis, MN: Resources for Adoptive Parents, 1997.

Spaulding for Children. Parents Are Tender Healers. National Resource for Adoptive Children. Detroit, 1996. Spaulding for Children. A National Adoption Strategic Plan. The Roundtable: Journal of the National Resource Center for Special Needs Adoption. Vol. 10, 2, 1996.

Steinhauer, Paul D. Assessing For Parental Capacity, American Orthopsychiatry. Vol. 53, 3, pp. 469-479, 1983.

Steinhauer, Paul D. The Least Detrimental Alternative. Toronto: University of Toronto Press, 1991.

Suderman, Abe and Graham, Wilf. Treatment Parent Rights. Blue Water Family Services, www.focis.com June, 1997.

Swan, Helen L. Treating Sexually Abused Children in Adoptive Families. Portland, ME: University of Southern Maine, 1993.

Taylor, Leah S. and Wendelbo, Lynn. Assessment & Treatment of Behaviorally

Troubled Children, Adolescents & Young Adults: A Manual & Working Book Using a Developmental Approach. Oklahoma City, OK: Wood 'N' Barnes Publishing & Distribution, 1997.

Weisman, Mary Lou. When Parents Are Not In The Best Interests Of The Child. The Atlantic Monthly. July, 1994.